Reading Critically about History:
A Guide to Active Reading

Rose Wassman
Lee Ann Rinsky

Prentice Hall, Upper Saddle River, New Jersey 07458

1998 by Prentice Hall, Inc.
mon & Schuster/A Viacom Company
pper Saddle River, New Jersey 07458

Printed in the United States of America
10 9 8 7 6 5 4 3

ISBN: 0-13-775636-4

Prentice-Hall International (UK) Limited, *London*
Prentice-Hall of Australia Pty. Limited, *Sydney*
Prentice-Hall Canada Inc., *Toronto*
Prentice-Hall Hispanoamericana, S.A., *Mexico*
Prentice-Hall of India Private Limited, *New Delhi*
Prentice-Hall of Japan, Inc., *Tokyo*
Simon & Schuster Pte. Ltd., *Singapore*
Editora Prentice-Hall do Brasil, Ltda., *Rio de Janeiro*

CONTENTS

CHAPTER 3   Identifying the Main Idea   27

CHAPTER 4   Recognizing Authors' Organizational Patterns   39

CHAPTER 5   Critical Thinking Skills   53

PREFACE

To the Student

If you read and carefully study the contents of this guidebook *before* you begin your first textbook reading assignment, you should have gained the skills and confidence needed to handle *any* college textbook effectively. This guidebook will enable you to learn quickly and efficiently. It is small in size but broad in scope. The writing style is intentionally simple and informal, so that you can easily learn what you need to know to get the most out of your textbook reading.

The secret of being a master student is to become an **active** reader who thinks along with the textbook author. An active reader is able to understand an author's ideas, to organize information so as to remember and use it, and to connect new ideas to ones already known. Reading is a thinking activity. Unless you can make sense out of what the author has stated, you have not "read" anything.

There are six chapters within this guidebook that focus on the skills needed to learn the essential information presented in college textbooks. In the first chapter, we show you how to become actively involved in the reading process by monitoring your comprehension and increasing your powers of concentration. You will learn an organized study system which will guarantee that you will not only understand what you read but also remember it!

You will learn, in the second chapter, how vocabulary skills aid comprehension and increase one's ability to read more quickly and will be introduced to the best strategies for understanding and remembering textbook terms.

In almost any reading that you do, understanding the main idea is essential. In chapter three, you will learn the best ways to identify and recall main ideas and to recognize major and minor details in passages.

By understanding how writers organize their ideas through specific patterns, you will learn, in Chapter Four, how to follow the flow of ideas in order to remember significant textbook information.

The heart of all reading is in analyzing what you read and thinking critically about what authors want you to know. You will learn how best to become an effective, critical reader in Chapter Five. Not only will you be able to make inferences readily, but you will see how logical reasoning leads to valid and sound conclusions. You will also learn the importance of recognizing an author's viewpoint, how words can carry implied meaning, and the significance of an author's tone and purpose.

In the last chapter, you will see the connection between critical reading and understanding visual aids in textbooks; knowing how to "read" them is invaluable in clarifying text information and recalling particular pertinent information.

We have included very short practices within some chapters. The real practice comes from applying the strategies presented here to your textbook. If you do so, you will become an active reader and learner. You may not always have to use *every* strategy you have learned and will find some strategies more suitable to your own particular learning style than others. We encourage you to be open-minded and to try *all* the strategies to find the ones that work best for you. Feel free to modify them and experiment with some learning techniques of your own. We hope that our goal of making your reading tasks easier will encourage you to become a life-long reader who finds joy and excitement in learning new things.

CHAPTER 1

Reading Actively

This guide to reading college textbooks will strengthen and enhance the ability you already have to comprehend and remember what you read. It focuses on those reading skills specifically needed to understand and critically evaluate the information in your textbooks. The guide will demonstrate that effective reading is more than a matter of developing one single skill. Rather, it involves a number of skills working together and strengthening one another. The essential skills you need for study-type-reading leading to effective critical thinking include:

vocabulary strategies
comprehension with retention
study strategies
critical thinking applications
effective use of textbook reading aids

BE AN ACTIVE READER

To be an effective reader, be an *active* reader—one who mentally engages in a dialogue with the writer. While reading, active readers agree and disagree, applaud and criticize, weigh and reconsider what the writer is saying. They involve themselves with the ideas, responding intellectually and/or emotionally to what they read. One prominent writer has stated that what he puts on paper is "a transaction" between himself and the reader, sharing who he is. Active readers involve themselves in that transaction, which in turn becomes a valuable aid to both improved concentration and comprehension.

CONCENTRATION-REMOVING DISTRACTIONS

Textbook reading is an information-getting process. Its primary activity is THINKING. Thinking demands concentration. Distractions while reading can interfere with concentration. Despite what may cause the distractions—removing them enhances your ability to concentrate. Reading for study-purposes leading to critical thinking demands your FULL attention.

Eliminating Distractions

Take care of such things as hunger or thirst before you begin any study session.

Create a quiet study environment for yourself.

Put aside temporarily any personal or emotional problems you may have.

Make your family members or roommates aware that you need *mental space* to study by removing any distractions, such as telephone or TV or loud music that may interfere with comprehension.

To further enhance your ability to concentrate and therefore improve your comprehension, have a positive attitude and be committed to learning about *history* well.

PREPARATION FOR READING: AN ORGANIZED STUDY SYSTEM

Some Common Misconceptions

A common misconception is that reading and study are identical processes. Reading—in preparation for study—is the process we use to understand the main idea of the textbook assignment. On the other hand, studying is the process we use to interpret, retain, and recall more detailed information, in order to answer questions, participate in class discussions, and succeed in tests or examinations.

A second misconception lies in how much time is needed to study a textbook, underestimating the time that *real* study involves. *Study steps are essential* in order to transfer what you have read and learned to your long-term memory. Using a study system enables you to study "smarter" and with greater efficiency.

STEP 1. PREPARING TO READ BY SURVEYING

You will be able to concentrate better, to understand and remember more, if you have a general idea of the contents of the textbook chapters. The key to study reading efficiently and gaining the needed background information, is to survey (sometimes called "to preview") a chapter. Surveying *makes you think* in advance about the subject, associating what you read with the world you live in. As you survey, think of some questions you might have to interact with the printed information and to set your "thinking gear" in motion.

The benefits of surveying cannot be overestimated. Surveying

1. leads to better comprehension and gives you a quick picture of the overall idea and some details.
2. helps you determine the organization of the chapter.
3. helps you note what parts of the material require a more careful reading.
4. is similar to consulting a map before leaving on a trip; you develop confidence because you know where you are going.

Surveying Procedure

When surveying, you will note that the writing pattern of many authors follows this sequence:

1. The topic may be suggested in the headings or subheadings.
2. The main idea may appear somewhere at the beginning of the section in the first, second, or third paragraph.
3. The remaining paragraphs support the main idea; and the conclusion often summarizes the main idea.

Surveying a textbook chapter is worth the five to fifteen minutes it takes. It enables you immediately to see the chapter as a whole and how various parts relate to the central idea. When surveying a textbook chapter, you

1. Check the OUTLINE of the chapter in the table of contents. This gives you a quick overview of the subject matter.
2. Return to the chapter and really THINK ABOUT THE TITLE, turning it into a question. For example, the title, The Renaissance: Economic and Political Rebirth, suggests the chapter will focus on politics during the renaissance, not culture or religion. Raise some additional questions about the chapter if you can. This should help you focus on the main points immediately, setting a purpose for the reading.
3. Look over the chapter's OBJECTIVES. This will give you a general idea of the key concepts.

4. Read the INTRODUCTION if there is one. In addition to needed background information, it may introduce you to the most important points.
5. Read any BOLDFACED HEADINGS and subheadings for each section you plan to study. Headings organize the information for you, outlining what is important.
6. Notice carefully the chapter's GRAPHIC AIDS: graphs, charts, diagrams, maps, tables, photographs, and cartoons. These often clarify concepts of a text concisely.
7. Note placement of the DEFINITION OF IMPORTANT WORDS—at the chapter's beginning or end. Usually, there is also a glossary of important terms. Familiarize yourself with the meaning of the important words/terms BEFORE you begin your actual reading.
8. Dip into the text here and there, SKIMMING the chapter. Skimming is quickly glancing over a chapter to determine structure, length, and format. <u>Read some of the first and last paragraph sentences,</u> familiarizing yourself with concepts the author will emphasize.
9. Read the SUMMARY or concluding paragraphs; these often restate the most important points covered in the chapter in brief form.
10. Read any QUESTIONS provided at the end of the chapter BEFORE reading the chapter, preparing you for what the author thinks is important and will stress.

An abbreviated example of steps 5 and 8 follows:

Mobilization, North and South

Neither side was prepared for a major war _____

_____

_____

War Fever _____

President Lincoln _____ mobilizing state militias _____

Lincoln's modest 90 day call up _____ General belief _____ war would

end quickly _____

_____

_____

Most soldiers were motivated by patriotism _____

_____

Enrollment Act, draft law _____ allowed for occupational exemptions

and for substitutions

Modifying Your Survey

Once you have completed your survey and before you begin your actual reading, ask yourself some general questions, such as

1. How familiar am I with this subject?
2. How should I divide up the sections and how much time do I need to read a section? the chapter?
3. What is important to know?
4. Are there key terms and words I need to master?

With any survey, it is likely you will have to modify your suggested procedure to accommodate the writer's style. Not all reading assignments have headings, visual aids, summaries or questions.

STEP 2. READ TO UNDERSTAND AND SELECT WHAT NEEDS TO BE REMEMBERED

The survey familiarizes you with some of the main points of the chapter, its specific purpose, and its organization. After you complete the survey, apply the following procedure to the first section, remembering to search for major concepts.

1. Read the entire section to get an overall view, actively searching for answers to questions you read or raised before reading, based on the title and survey.
2. Think only about what is really important. Do not dwell on trivial details.
3. Selectively mark your textbook as you read. Have a pen or pencil in hand, placing marginal symbols next to key lines. Develop a simple coding system for these marks, such as

> = (main idea)   —- (important support)   * (important)
> 1, 2, 3 (specific points to recall)   K (key term)
> ex. (example)   ? (difficult)

Read the entire section before underlining, highlighting, or making extensive marginal notes. After you make your original brief marginal markings, you will have a better idea as to what is important. Initially everything may seem important, but after reading the entire section, you should realize this is untrue. Do not underline or highlight too much—you might as well not underline at all! Be selective and underline in thought units, using key words and phrases.

Try to say aloud in your own words what you understand to be the answers to questions you have posed and also what you have gained from the reading. Connect the key points that have been stressed. Remember, the most important question to keep asking is:

What does the author want me to know, that is, what is important here?

Following is a brief example of initial markings.

Relief

Roosevelt also provided relief for the unemployed. The **Federal Emergency Relief Administration (FERA)** provided funds to state and local agencies. Harry Hopkins, who had headed Roosevelt's relief program in New York, became its director. Soon he was one of the New Deal's most important members and lived in the White House as a confidant of both Franklin and Eleanor. FERA spent over $3 billion before it ended in 1935, and by then Hopkins and FDR had developed new programs that provided work rather than just cash. Work relief, they believed, preserved both the skills and the morale of recipients. In the winter of 1933–1934, Hopkins spent nearly $1 billion to create jobs for 4 million men and women through the **Civil Works Administration (CWA)**. The CWA hired laborers to build roads and airports, teachers to staff rural schools and adult education programs, and singers and artists to give public performances. Another relief agency,

= relief for unemployed ex. FERA

---three billion spent by FERA

= work relief

ex. CWA built roads etc. . .

the **Public Works Administration (PWA)**, provided work relief on useful projects to stimulate the
economy through public expenditures. Directed by
Harold Ickes, the PWA spent billions from 1933 to
1939 to build schools, hospitals, courthouses,
airports, dams, and bridges.

     ex. PWA

    One of FDR's personal ideas, the **Civilian
Conservation Corps (CCC)**, combined work relief
with conservation. Launched in March 1933, the
CCC employed 2.5 million young men to work on
reforestation and flood control projects, build roads
and bridges in national forests and parks, restore
Civil War battlefields, and fight forest fires. The
men lived in isolated CCC camps in exchange for
$30 a month, $25 of which had to be sent home.
"I'd go anywhere," said one Baltimore applicant.
"I'd go to hell if I could get work there." One of the
most popular New Deal agencies, the CCC lasted
till 1942.

     ex. CCC; work relief and conservation

     ---lived in isolated camps

STEP 3 RESTATE AND ORGANIZE THE INFORMATION TO RETAIN IT

Most students wish they could read their textbook assignments once, and
highlight or underline while reading, and remember everything they read.
Although this is not possible, following Step 3 will enable you to retain
much more of what you read. When you find a logical or natural break,
after you have read several pages, paraphrase, or restate the ideas in your
own words, so as to strengthen your concentration. This shows what you
remember, a sure way to test what you have understood and learned.

    The form of organization you choose depends on your familiarity
with the reading material, your learning style, and the type of textbook
you are reading. You may choose to use notetaking, write an abbreviated
outline, answer some key questions, write notes on index cards, create a
divided page, or map important concepts.

    Remember, you must restate the material in your own words and
"make" the knowledge yours by paraphrasing in order to retain it. Be
certain, also, that in organizing your information, you have included some
of the important supporting details.

WAYS TO RESTATE AND ORGANIZE INFORMATION

Several strategies can help make ideas your own and help you remember them.

Simplified Outline

Outlining is an organized form of note taking. With most textbooks, you can see quickly how key ideas are related to each other by noting the headings and subheadings, using them as a guide. Simply

— List in order only main ideas or main headings, relating the subheadings and major details.
— Indent to separate important points.
— Use phrases, omit unnecessary words, and abbreviate when possible.

Example of Simplified Outline
Relief for unemployed
    FERA direct funds for states and localities
        Harry Hopkins Director
        spent 3 billion by 1935

    Moved to work relief
        CWA one billion dollars for four million jobs
            built roads, taught school, artists etc. . .
        PWA spent billions between 1933 and 1939
            work relief to stimulate economy
            built schools, hospitals etc. . .
        CCC FDR's personal idea
            combined work relief with conservation
            2.5 million lived in isolated camps for $30 per month
            popular agency, lasted until 1942

Using Cards

Although it is easier to underline and write notes in the margin of your text, sometimes you are unable to do so. There are other alternatives for study. You can use index cards and write your restatement notes after reading each section. Use the lined side, and, on the blank side, write the chapter heading or subheading. Number the cards so they are organized and write a summary card.

Example of a Study Card

Unemployment Relief
Direct Relief
  FERA-provided funds for state and local agencies
       headed by Harry Hopkins
       spent 3 billion by 1935

Work Relief
  CWA-spent 1 billion for 4 million jobs in 1933–34
      built roads and buildings
      teachers for rural schools
      employed artists and performers
  PWA-spent billions between 1933–39
      work relief designed to stimulate the economy
      built schools, hospitals
  CCC-FDR's personal idea
      combined work relief with conservation
      2.5 million lived in isolated camps and worked for $30 per month
      popular New Deal agency, lasted until 1942

The Divided Page

The divided page, or Cornell method, is still another way to organize for study. In one column of a page, record important questions to answer or key concepts or terms to learn. As you study, jot the answer or information in the column to the right. The dividing line makes it possible to fold your answers underneath or cover them completely as you study. This method is often used together with other methods, such as mapping, which follows.

Example of a Divided Page

Relief for the Unemployed

Direct Relief

FERA	Provided funds for state and local agencies headed by Harry Hopkins spent 3 billion by 1935
Shift to work relief	
CWA	spent 1 billion for 4 million jobs in 1933–34 built roads and buildings provided teachers for local schools and employed artists
PWA	spent billions between 1933–39 work relief designed to stimulate the economy built schools, hospitals etc. . .
CCC	FDR's personal idea combined work relief with conservation 2.5 million lived in isolated camps and worked popular agency, lasted until 1942

Mapping

Mapping is the creation of a graphic chart or word picture so that all pertinent information is visible at one time. The major and minor supporting information to remember is placed in a form that resembles a map or chart, hence the term. For some students, this visualization enables them to recall the textual information much more readily and stimulate "creative thinking."

Most chapters divide into three or four major sections. You can map each section separately, or if there are many small headings, you can sometimes combine them into one map. When mapping a textbook chapter, you can proceed initially by

1. Surveying the chapter, then previewing each section.
2. Reading, marking, and organizing the important parts.
3. Producing the map, as explained below.

Guidelines for Mapping

1. Write the main chapter section or title in the center of the paper and build the rest of the information around it.

2. To highlight the main chapter section, draw a square or circle or any other shape around it.

3. Add key words that express the major points. Write these points as branches off the central hub and box or circle them. If the selection is already divided into labeled sections, your task is easy. If there are no divisions, you must group and label the information.

4. Complete the map by adding minor important details off the branches. Try to do some of this from memory.

5. Use larger print for important ideas, decreasing size with items of lesser importance. Turn your paper sideways so you can use the width of the paper for your major headings.

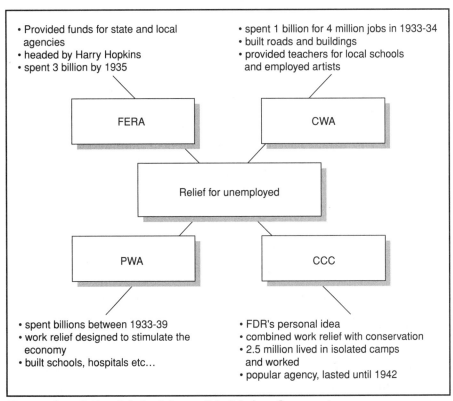

Example of the Main Idea with Major Support

The survey and markings or underlining should be done before mapping so that you reduce the information placed on the map to key ideas. You are creating a study guide so that, before a quiz, you need only spend a brief amount of review time. Moreover, while you are creating the map, you are actually doing further organizing, reconstructing for yourself what needs to be remembered in their order of importance.

Frequently, students use mapping in conjunction with the divided page. They place the vocabulary they need to remember, or particular details, on the divided page. This prevents the map from becoming too cluttered. With mapping, you want to show the relationships so details can be more easily visualized and recalled.

An additional mapping technique that aids retention is to use color, separating important ideas and details. Color is a powerful linking device that can help you remember related information.

A Final Step with All Study Systems: A Summary

The final step with all study systems is to write a good summary of the chapter. Summaries are brief statements about the material you have read. Writing summaries is an excellent study technique to help you think actively about the information and help you determine whether you understand the material. Also, they enable you to remember the information *because you restate it in your own words*.

With all summaries, first write a general statement of the main idea. Show the *connection* between the main idea and support. Avoid unnecessary words and include only the most important details. Write your summary in an organized way. If necessary, use some connecting words such as *first, second, additionally*.

To summarize difficult text material, you can first mark your text and

1. Circle the topic or subject.
2. Highlight or underline key ideas and then combine them when you write.
3. Cross out unimportant details or unnecessary and redundant information.
4. Create a topic sentence which explains the overall key idea. Add only the major details.

Here is an example of a summary of some of the text information you have just analyzed.

Unemployment Relief

Unemployment Relief

The New Deal provided for relief for the unemployed first by giving money to the states through the FERA. Headed by Harry Hopkins it spent three billion before it ended in 1935.

Direct public works programs then emerged. The CWA hired laborers, teachers and artists and created jobs for them. During the winter of 1933–34 it spent one billion dollars. The PWA sought to provide work relief that would stimulate the economy. It spent billions to build schools roads, hospitals etc. . .

FDR's personal idea, the CCC, combined work relief with conservation employing 2.5 million men in outdoor projects. They lived in isolated camps and worked for $30 per month. It was a popular program and lasted until 1942.

CHAPTER 2

Vocabulary Strategies
to Aid Comprehension

The best way to increase your vocabulary is TO READ. As this guide will show you, reading well and developing a strong vocabulary are interrelated. The more words you know, the better and faster you can understand what you read. Textbook writers introduce you to many new words and much of mastering a subject is mastering its vocabulary. For example, *gerrymander* and *privatization* are terms you might find in a government, business, history, or political science textbook. To read confidently, you need a method to "figure out," or deduce, the meaning of words and terms you read but do not understand.

VOCABULARY STRATEGIES

Some Things to Avoid

Generally, you have a huge amount of reading to do outside of classes. No doubt, you encounter many unfamiliar and seemingly difficult words. College texts usually contain terms specific to their subject but looking up their meanings in the dictionary is not necessarily the BEST strategy to use. If your tendency is to look up every unfamiliar word in a dictionary, DON'T. Chances are you will soon be overwhelmed with both the time it takes and the distraction in your comprehension. Also, it is difficult to remember every word you look up in the dictionary. Additionally, the dictionary may list many meanings for just one word. Which one should you choose? Remember that while the dictionary is an important learning tool, it is not the only, nor even the first, approach to use in finding a word's meaning.

Memorizing lists of words also does not necessarily increase your vocabulary. Rote learning of words—memorizing by repetition *without understanding*—makes it difficult to remember them. Often, the concept or ideas of the word and its general context (**where** it is used) are as important as its stated definition.

STRATEGIES THAT CAN HELP

There is no instantaneous way to acquire a superior vocabulary. Certain strategies, however, can help you master college textbook words.

1. Learn to use the context efficiently, the BEST way.
2. Use the word's structure (prefixes, suffixes, and roots) you already know and apply them to unknown words.
3. Develop a *systematic* way to collect words you read and hear but whose meaning is unclear.
4. Use memory devices, known as *mnemonics,* to visualize word meanings, associating the meanings with something you know.
5. Use the dictionary to help you pronounce words and more fully understand their meanings. Pronouncing words helps you retain their meaning.

Using the Context—A Powerful Strategy

Textbook authors usually define important terms; you can often determine the meanings of words by how they are used in a sentence. As you read, inferring the meaning of a word according to how it is used is a part of critical thinking. The context of a sentence—the word or words surrounding an unknown word—aids in determining the unknown word's meaning. Additionally, a word's meaning is clearly dependent upon *how it is used in a sentence.* Using the sentence context is, in part, *guessing intelligently* about a word's meaning. Your guess cannot be a wild one, but rather an educated guess, based on clear and serious thinking and on the information the writer has provided.

Note, for example, how a simple word such as *bank* has its meaning strictly determined by its use in the sentence:

She placed all her money in the **bank.** (a place to deposit money)
The river**bank** overflowed from the storm. (the earth side of a river)
A plane appeared out of the fog, **banked,** and stopped (tilted and caused to turn)

Kinds of Context Clues Most Commonly Found in Textbooks

Direct Explanation

The direct explanation, or definition clue, is the easiest clue to spot, and the most commonly used in textbooks. Some authors simply tell you directly what a word means, using signal words such as *that is*, *is defined as*, or simply *is*.

> As historians present their differing interpretations, each tries to mount the most persuasive arguments, marshaling **primary source** materials, that is materials from contemporary participants in the events; **secondary sources**, that is, later comments on the consequences of the events; and appeals to the sensibilities of the reader.
>
> Howard Spodek, *The World's History*

> A **society** is a group of people organized together so that their needs--the sustaining of life at the most basic level--can be met.
>
> Gary B. Nash, *Red White, and Black*

Example

Often, the author will give examples that relate to a word to clarify it.

> . . .the *Era of Good Feelings*, an expression that nicely captured the spirit of political harmony and sectional unity that washed over the republic in the immediate postwar years. National pride surged with the humbling of the British at New Orleans, the demise of the Federalists lessened political tensions, and the economy boomed.
>
> David Goldfield, et al., *The American Journey*

Examples are sometimes used to point out instances, characteristics, or illustrations. Signal words such as *like*, and *for instance* may or may not be used.

> *Like* other storytellers, the ancient Greek bards did not memorize their poems exactly. They had, however, a repertory of especially apt, fixed phrases that could be used to fill out a line or give a singer time to remember the next episode in his story.
>
> William McNeill, *A History of the Human Community*

Past Experience—Making an Educated Guess

You can use your own familiarity with situations to help understand or clarify a word.

> On the basis of humankinds moral sense, Kant <u>postulated</u> the existence of God, eternal life, and future rewards and punishments.
>
> Donald Kagan et al., The Western Heritage

(Does <u>postulated</u> mean theorized or proved?)

> Students for a Democratic Society (SDS) <u>epitomized</u> the early new left.
>
> David Goldfield et al., The American Journey

(Does <u>epitomized</u> mean represented or rejected?)

Using Word Structure

What Is Word Structure?

Another way to determine the meaning of many textbook words readily is to acquire a general knowledge of how words are structured—to learn to use these word parts: prefixes, roots, and suffixes. Many of these word parts derive from Latin and Greek and make up the structure of most academic textbook words. Using these word parts goes hand-in-hand with using context clues. Word part meanings usually give you a GENERAL sense of a word's meaning, while context makes the meaning more SPECIFIC.

The Three Word Parts

Let's examine how each word part functions:

Prefix: *Pre* means before. The prefix (a group of letters) always comes *before* the main part of the word and <u>changes</u> the word's meaning.

use **re**use   place **mis**place   sure **un**sure

Root: All words must have a root or stem. It is the main part of the word and carries the basic meaning of the word.

vitamin   **vita**lity   re**vita**lize   (vita = life)

Suffix: The suffix (a group of letters) comes *after* the main part of a word. The suffix indicates what part of speech the word is, that is, whether it is a noun, verb, adjective, or adverb. Most suffixes carry only limited word meaning.

amaze   amaze**ment** (n)   nation   nation**al** (adj.)
special   special**ize**) (v)   rare   rare**ly** (adv.)

Note: Suffixes are not as helpful as prefixes in guessing word meanings. Many suffixes have a rather "generic" meaning such as "related to." Unlike prefixes, suffixes rarely change the basic meaning of the word but rather alter the word's part of speech, the suffix's major role.

The following brief chart shows how these word parts may change meaning or part of speech.

Prefix	Root/or Root Word	New Word and Part of Speech	Suffix	New Word and New Part of Speech
pre (*means before*)	dict(*meaning speak*)	predict (v)	tion (n)	prediction (n)
mis (*means wrong*)	judge	misjudge (v)	ment (n)	misjudgment (n)
re (*means again*)	place	replace (v)	able (adj.)	replaceable (adj.)
dis (*means not*)	obedient	disobedient (adj.)	ly (adv.)	disobediently (adv.)

Remember, however, that you will come across unfamiliar words, not in isolation as in these words, but when you are reading. In your textbook, these words will be used in the context of sentences and paragraphs. Your use of context clues AND knowledge of word parts together may give you a good idea of the word's meaning.

Commonly Used Word Parts

Memorizing long lists of prefixes, roots, and suffixes is not necessary unless you have an extraordinary amount of free time. Try to get the essence of the meaning of the most commonly used word parts through the categories in which they are grouped. The following charts list some of the most commonly used word parts.

Prefixes

1. Learn the prefixes that suggest something negative or that can mean "not."

WORD PART	MEANING	EXAMPLE
anti	against	antifreeze
dis	not; opposite	disown; disconnect
in	not	inactive; incorrect
mis	wrong	misadventure
non	not	nonessential
un	not	unavailable

2. Learn the prefixes that change time.

post	after	postgraduate
pre	before	preconditions
re	again	reactivate
retro	back	retrograde

3. Learn the prefixes that concern placement or direction.

circum	around	circumnavigate
ex or e	out of	expand; eject
inter	between	interview
intra	within	intrastate
per	through	perspire
pro	forward	propeller
sub	below	subnormal
super	above	superhuman
trans	across	transportation

4. Learn the prefixes that refer to numbers.

uni	one	universe
bi	two	bilateral (agreement)
tri	three	triad
deca	ten	decathlon
cent	hundred	centigrade

Roots

5. Learn the important roots.

bio	life	bionics
cide	to kill	genocide
dic (dict)	to speak	dictator
graph	write	graphite; cardiogram
ology	study	microbiology
path	feeling; suffering	pathologist

| scrib | to write | transcribe |
| vita | life | revitalize |

Suffixes

6. Learn the **noun** suffixes. Noun suffixes are the <u>most common</u> in textbooks since they name things. Their meaning is something like "the state of," "the quality of," "related to"

WORD PART	WORD ROOT	EXAMPLE
ance	attend (v)	attendance
ence	prefer (v)	preference
ion	agitate (v)	agitation
ism	social (adj.)	socialism
ity; ty	superior (adj.)	superiority; loyalty
ment	agree (v)	agreement
ness	great (adj.)	greatness

All These Example Words Are Nouns

7. Learn the few **verb** suffixes

ate	stimulus (n)	stimulate
ize	drama (n)	dramatize
ify	class (n)	classify

These Example Words Are Verbs

8. Learn some **adjective** suffixes. A few have some meaning.

able; ible (*capable of*)	accept (v) sense (n)	acceptable; sensible
ful (*full of*)	beauty (n)	beautiful
less (*without*)	shape (n)	shapeless
ous (*full of*)	courage (n)	courageous

These Example Words Are Adjectives

Adverb suffixes are simply adjective suffixes to which *ly* has been added. *acceptably, sensibly, beautifully,* and *courageously.*

We mentioned that since textbooks often name things, many important words appear as nouns. Simple verbs such as *defend* can become the noun, *defendant,* and simple adjectives such as *sober* become more difficult to recognize as *sobriety.* When you encounter any of these more complex word form, try to figure out the term from its simple root. This will help you determine the word's meaning.

STRATEGIES FOR REMEMBERING TEXTBOOK VOCABULARY

Having determined the meanings of unfamiliar words as you read does not necessarily mean you will remember them. There is a difference between deducing definitions as you read and *learning* them. Remember that many of these same words will appear on your courses' quizzes and exams. To learn words, you can draw upon several options to help you master their meanings:

a personal word bank of vocabulary cards or a personalized list visualization and association techniques.

A Personal Word Bank: Vocabulary Cards

Have a number of 3 × 5 index cards ready to copy key terms when reading; also, take some to class to jot down important lecture terms you hear. Construct your sample card like this.

1. On the front side of the card, neatly write or print in large letters the word you want to remember and the part of speech.
2. Beneath it, write the **phonetic** spelling to help you with pronunciation.
3. Beneath that, copy the context phrase or sentence in which the word appeared. This phrase/sentence will help jog your memory and help you to retain the meaning of the word.
4. On the back of the card, write a short definition of the word, the definition that applies to the phrase or sentence context.
5. Beneath the definition, write a sentence of your own, using the word.

Students generally like the personal vocabulary-card system because they only study the words they need to learn at any time, anywhere. Since the cards are small and portable, you can carry them around with you whether on campus, at home, or even running errands. You can reorder them by category or subject.

To practice, start by looking at the word, saying it aloud, and trying to tell yourself the definition. The act of recitation begins to lock the word's meaning in your memory bank, activating your thinking process. As you check your memory, by looking at the back of the card, make two groups: place the cards you know immediately and feel confident about in one group and place those you need more practice within the other group. Continue studying the difficult ones until all the cards are in the "I Know It" group. Shuffle the cards and do a final practice.

Sample–Front Side of a Vocabulary Card

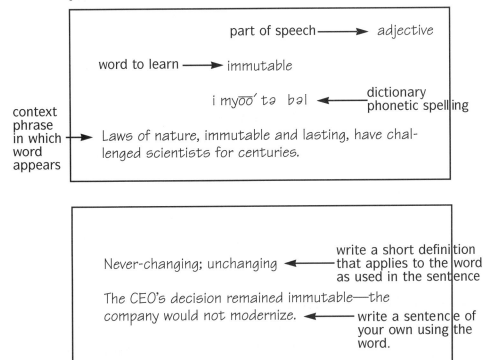

Sample–Back Side of a Vocabulary Card

A Personalized List

Just as you can create vocabulary cards, you might want to consider using your computer to develop a master list of words by subject. The computer permits greater flexibility, allowing you to move words and categories around the screen. You should experiment with making several vocabulary cards and also a personalized list to see which method best suits your learning style. Once this is determined, use either method; it's not necessary to do both!

Using Mnemonics, or Memory Devices

Visualization and Association

Two principles of memory training apply in learning unfamiliar words: visualize the information and associate the word with something you know. Remember,

1. the mind can think in pictures.

2. it is always easier to remember things that have meaning than to remember things that do not. Association with something known helps in memory retention.

Mnemonics, that is, a memory trick, helps you remember a word and depends on vivid associations and the ability to visualize.

Think of a word like *jounce* (pronounced jouns).
It refers to the compression of a suspension spring (auto tech term).
Jounce sounds like bounce. When something bounces, it springs.

Once you have made an association, try to form a visual image of the word and definition you want to remember. Exaggerating the image somewhat helps you recall it more easily. Try to draw on your own personal experience when you make associations and visualize images; the more personal you make the mnemonic, the easier it will be to remember the word.

Noting and Marking Words for Study

Textbook writers might include a glossary, a list of key terms and their meaning, printed either at the end of each chapter or at the back of the book. Most importantly, authors write in such a way as to help you understand concepts and key terms, often emphasizing important words with **boldface** print or *italics*.

If the author has given you the exact definition of an unknown term, or if you have deduced the meaning from context clues, it is a good idea to mark it in some way in your text to help you remember it.

Sometimes glossary terms, written in academic language, must be "translated" by you into everyday English as illustrated by the italics in the definitions below.

Nonintercourse Act	a measure that prohibited American Trade only with Britain and France (*ended total embargo*)
underground railroad	a secret network of stations and safe houses organized by Quakers and other anti-slavery people (*north to freedom!*)
Monroe Doctrine	policy in which Europe would stay out of the Americas and the U.S. would stay out of European affairs (*everyone minds his own business!*)

These are a number of useful marking options for these words:

1. highlighting
2. circling
3. underlining with color
4. making a marginal symbol, such as an asterisk

Make certain to include the author's definition in your notation.

The Dictionary

You may not always be able to figure out a word's meaning from the context or the word parts and may need to use the dictionary. The key to using a dictionary successfully is to be aware of the aids it provides and to understand its organization.

Pitfalls in Using a Dictionary

1. The first given definition is not necessarily the meaning you are seeking. Many words have more than one meaning since most dictionary writers try to include all the possible definitions for a word. It is important to THINK about how the word was used when you came across it in your reading. Then, select the appropriate meaning from the choices given. When students are in a hurry to get through the text, they often select the first definition they see. For example, two of five definitions of the word **sanctions** would appear this way in the dictionary:

   1: <u>authorized approval</u> or permission . . . 5. (a) a coercive measure as <u>a blockade</u> of a shipment usually taken by several nations together to force a demand. 5. (b) a coercive measure as a <u>boycott.</u>

   Obviously, selecting the definition of approval instead of *block-ade* or *boycott* would lead to a false interpretation of the sentence and paragraph.

2. Sometimes, a word is explained with another word whose meaning is also unclear. Don't just memorize a word's meaning without understanding it fully. For example, the dictionary's first definition of the word **garrulous** is

   1: given to prosy, rambling, or tediously loquacity

   but the second definition (2. wordy, talkative) is much clearer, and the word **garrulous** is readily understood.

In addition to the importance of learning vocabulary strategies to aid comprehension, in the next chapter, we will examine how to avoid comprehension problems in identifying the main idea and supporting details.

CHAPTER 3

Identifying the Main Idea

DISTINGUISHING THE TOPIC FROM THE MAIN IDEA

The topic of a passage differs from the main idea. A common error made by some readers is to equate the topic of a paragraph or passage with the main idea. The *topic* is the subject of a paragraph or passage and is most general in nature. On the other hand, *the main idea makes a particular statement or emphasizes a special aspect of the topic*. The topic may be stated in a word or short phrase and may often be mentioned over and over again, whereas the main idea is usually expressed as a complete thought.

If a textbook author wanted to focus on the topic "the Constitution," for example, the author could emphasize any of the following aspects:

1. Conflicts in the development of the Constitution
2. The major provisions of the Constitution
3. The changes in Constitutional interpretation over time.

Simply asking "What is it about?" can help you determine the topic. For example, with each of the above titles, the answer to "What is it about?" would be "the Constitution." That would be the topic but *not* the main idea.

How Supporting Details Help Reveal the Topic

Many of the passage's specific supporting details should also help you form an impression that will reveal the topic. The support can take the form of examples, reasons, statistics, explanation, or simply relevant information. To see how this works, study the following example of a topic, its main idea, and specific support.

Topic: Political and social protest in the 60's and 70's
Main Idea: Radicals in the 1950's laid the groundwork for protest in the 60's and 70's by breaking new intellectual ground.

27

Support: (A) The poetry of Allen Ginsberg denounced materialism and middle-class morality.

(B) The Sociologist C. Wright Mills wrote that an undemocratic power elite dominated American society.

(C) Paul Goodman claimed that liberal institutions repressed young Americans.

STRATEGIES TO USE IN FINDING THE MAIN IDEA

Several strategies can be used to find and understand the main idea, the chief ones being

1. Asking key questions about the paragraph's content.
2. Locating a general statement within the paragraph that expresses the author's message.
3. Noting how the sum of the details emphasizes a main point.

We can begin finding the main idea by making use of what we have learned about the topic, and then asking, "What important thing is being said about the topic?" or "What is happening to the topic?" Words, phrases, or ideas that are repeated are *clues* to answering this question. Underlining these clues can sometimes help you see a main idea almost immediately.

Next, ask yourself, "How much support does the writer give for this idea?" The amount of detail and support mentioned by the writer will give you a general impression of his or her overall point. Remember, the writer can use examples, reasons, and situations to help develop or support the main point.

Let's examine how these questions can be applied to finding the main idea in the following paragraph.

Britain continued through much of the nineteenth century to be the home of aggressive entrepeneurs and ingenious inventors. It produced more efficient steam engines and larger textile mills, new applications of steam power to transportation and new processes for the smelting of steel. Though much of the country remained rural, Britain continued to be the most heavily industrialized of nations and to enjoy the highest per capita income of all the Western powers. Only at the end of the century was the predominance challenged—by nations that had acquired much of their industrial know-how from the British.

Anthony Esler, *The Western World*

Answer the following questions in the space provided.

1. Who or what is the paragraph about? What is the topic?

The topic is _____

2. What is stated about the topic? What is the topic's specific focus?

The topic's specific focus is _____

The combined answers to these questions give you the author's main point: In the nineteenth century, Britain was an aggressive entrepreneurial and industrial nation.

Although the author stated the main idea precisely in the first sentence, we have paraphrased it—changed several of the words and the word order. All the remaining sentences of this paragraph that deal with Britain's industrial spirit support the first sentence and answer a third key question.

With what specific details does the author support his point?

3. Copy two supporting statements.

a. _____

b. _____

FINDING THE MAIN IDEA IN A TEXTBOOK PARAGRAPH

With most paragraphs, there is often one sentence that specifically states the main idea directly as in the previous paragraph: *"Britain was an aggressive enterpreneurial . . . ."* The main idea may be found in different places in a paragraph, but it is usually found in the first or last paragraph sentence. Sometimes, however, if introductory material is presented, the main idea may be stated in the second or a later sentence. In a few instances, it may be scattered in phrases or sentences throughout the paragraph. And, finally, writers may not state a main idea directly but imply it instead, requiring the reader to draw a conclusion on the basis of other statements. Main ideas that are implied, that is, suggested rather than stated explicitly, are sometimes more difficult to isolate. In these cases, a summary of the paragraph's details can often help in pinpointing an implied main idea.

First and Last Sentence Main Idea

In textbooks, in about 60 percent of the time, the first sentence of the paragraph contains the main idea. Study the following paragraph for an illustration of a first sentence main idea. The *topic* is circled, the *main idea* sentence is underlined, and the *supporting statements* are italicized to help you recognize all three facets of the paragraph.

> In the early twentieth century, (progressive reformers) responded to the tensions of industrial and urban development by moving to change society and government. Rejecting an earlier emphasis on individualism and laissez-faire, *they organized to promote social change and an interventionist state.* Programs and *laws to protect women, children, and injured workers testified to their compassion;* the *creation of new agencies and political techniques indicated their interest in order and efficiency;* campaigns to end corruption, whether perceived in urban political machines, corporate influence, drunkenness, or "inferior" immigrants, illustrated their self-assured vision of the public good.
>
> David Goldfield et al., *The American Journey*

Rather than state the main idea at the beginning of a paragraph, some writers conclude a paragraph with the main idea sentence. A concluding sentence often emphasizes how strongly the writer feels about an idea. Thus, the author presents supporting information at the beginning of the paragraph, leading you to the main idea in the final sentence.

> Yet a (reaction against Western imperialism was setting in.) A mass uprising was underway in Egypt. A determined nationalist resistance movement was gaining momentum among the Turks. *Iranians were standing their ground against the Anglo-Iranian Treaty.* Iraq was in revolt. Amir Abdullah was threatening to avenge his brother Faysal's expulsion from Syria. Anti-Zionist riots were beginning in Palestine. Even in countries where nationalism appeared to have been crushed during the summer of 1920, it would, in most cases, achieve partial success within the next two years.
>
> Glenn Perry, *The Middle East*

Restated Main Idea in First and Last Sentence

Sometimes, writers help their readers grasp the main point by restating it at the end of a paragraph even though it was stated in the beginning. Read the following paragraph and then answer the questions.

If you concentrate on each separate word while reading, you create comprehension problems for yourself. In addition, often you may find that after you read a passage you cannot recall much of it. Research shows that in just one second, the brain can sort out 100 million separate messages, distinguishing between the important and the unimportant. The inefficient reader sends to the brain such "weak signals"—seemingly unrelated chunks of information—that the brain loses its focus on reading and gets distracted or bored. The eyes look at the print but the brain wanders: thinking, planning, daydreaming about unrelated topics. If you are unable to concentrate while reading or become easily bored or restless, you are probably reading too slowly to engage your mind in the reading material.

Wassman/Rinsky *Effective Reading in a Changing World*

1. What is the topic? _____

2. What main point is made about the topic?_____

3. What information is given in support of the main idea? _____

Main Idea in the Middle

Sometimes, the writer first makes a broad statement or begins with a quotation or question, particularly when the main idea is stated in the second or third sentence.

Was the collapse of the constitutional monarchy inevitable? If so, why? *Critics have pointed to some shortcomings in the design of the 1791 Constitution that helped hasten its demise.* The logic of national sovereignty may have favored the idea of a one-house legislature, but practical experience in France and elsewhere has suggested that a bicameral system provides for more thorough airing of controversies and more careful legislation. Giving the king the power to delay legislation with the suspensive veto but not to reject it altogether made him the target of protests if he opposed popular proposals, but it didn't give him real authority to defend his point of view. Even so, the internal flaws of the constitution were not so obvious as to make it unworkable. Experience in a number of European countries during the nineteenth century demonstrated that constitutional monarchy could be a successful form of government, capable of evolving in the direction of fuller democracy.

Jeremy Popkin, *A Short History of the French Revolution*

Also, some authors begin with a statement to help create interest and get the reader involved before making the main point. As you read the following paragraph, you may wish to circle words that are clues to the topic and underline some of the supporting details to help you find the precise main idea statement. Then, answer the questions that follow.

Between June 10 and September 22, 1692, nineteen people were hanged for witchcraft in Salem, Massachusetts. One man was pressed to death, and over 150 others from twenty-four towns and villages went to jail, where four adults and one infant died and some remained until the following May. Compared to other witch hunts in the Western world, it was a minor affair, or as one historian has put it, "a small incident in the history of a great superstition."[1] It was the largest of its kind in the British colonies of North America, however, and it has never lost its grip on either the popular or scholarly imagination.

Bryan LeBeau, *The Story of the Salem Witch Trials*

Topic: _____

Main idea: _____

Supporting statement: _____

Legend spoke of the Comstock Lode and the silver veins of the Sierras. In Colorado, gold was to be found and placer miners spread along a thousand miles of the Rockies south from British Columbia. Across Americans' memory plod hard-bitten prospectors, staking their claims. Actually, it took eastern capital and big money to make mining pay. With enough funds, hydraulic mining could bring veins to the surface by firing a high-pressure stream of water at them. Hillsides broke apart and the debris poured into long sluices that were then sifted through for minerals of value. Hard-rock mining lasted longer, but it took patience, time, and plenty of capital. Driving a shaft, and buying beams and posts to shore the tunnels, pumps to draw water out of the shaft, and hoists to carry the ore all required an outlay from the Pacific coast's cities and eastern banks.

Mark Summers, *The Gilded Age*

Topic: _____

Main idea: _____

Supporting statement: _____

Main Idea Scattered throughout the Paragraph

In the following selection, the main point is scattered throughout the paragraph. As you read, sort out what is most important. Then reread and underline the key words which, when pieced together, form the main idea. In the space provided, write a sentence or two, stating the main point in your own words.

The Scopes "monkey trial"—so called because fundamentalists trivialized Darwin's theory into a claim that humans were descended from monkeys—became one of the most publicized and definitive moments of the decade. The real drama was the confrontation between Darrow and Bryan. Darrow, denied the right to call scientists to testify for the defense, put "the Great Commoner," Bryan, himself on the stand as an expert witness on the Bible. Bryan delighted his supporters with a staunch defense of biblical literalism. But he also drew scorn from many of the assembled journalists, including cosmopolitan types such as H. L. Mencken of the *Baltimore Sun*, who ridiculed Bryan's simplistic faith. Scopes's guilt was never in question. The jury convicted him quickly, although the verdict was later thrown out on a technicality. Bryan died a week after the trial; his epitaph read simply, "He kept the Faith." The struggle over the teaching of evolution continued in an uneasy stalemate; state statutes were not repealed, but prosecutions ceased. Fundamentalism, a religious creed and a cultural defense against the uncertainties of modern life, continued to have a strong appeal for millions of Americans.

David Goldfield et al., *The American Journey*

Main idea: _____

_____

UNDERSTANDING THE IMPLIED MAIN IDEA

In a few paragraphs, you may have to supply the main idea if the author does not state it directly. This requires that you draw a conclusion based on the supporting statements that have been made. Read the following paragraph. Think about the topic and what the author is saying about it; then, write the implied main idea in the space provided.

Alexander Graham Bell thought the telephone should properly be answered by saying, "Hoy! Hoy!"—an odd term from the Middle English that became the sailor's "ahoy!" and reflected Bell's sense that those speaking on early telephones were meeting like ships on a lonely and vast electronic sea. The world has now grown electronically dense, densest of all perhaps among the Japanese, who answer the telephone with a crowded, tender, almost cuddling quick-whispered *mushi-mushi*. The Russians say *slushaiyu* (I'm listening). The hipper Russians say *allo*, Italians say *pronto* (ready). The Chinese say *wei, wei* (with a pause between the words, unlike the Japanese mushi-mushi).

Lance Morrow, *Time*

Main idea: _____

_____

_____

Pleading the Fifth Amendment

The Fifth Amendment to the U.S. Constitution is one of the best known entries in the Bill of Rights. Television shows and crime novels have popularized phrases such as "pleading the Fifth," or "taking the Fifth." As these media recognize, the Fifth Amendment is a powerful ally of any criminal defendant. When the accused, generally upon the advice of counsel, decides to invoke the Fifth Amendment right against self-incrimination, the state cannot require the defendant to testify. In the past, defendants who refused to take the stand were often denigrated by comments the prosecution made to the jury. In 1965 the U.S. Supreme Court, in the case of *Griffin v. California*, ruled that the defendant's unwillingness to testify could not be interpreted as a sign of guilt. The Court reasoned that such interpretations forced the defendant to testify and effectively negated Fifth Amendment guarantees. Defendants who choose to testify, however, but who fail to adequately answer the questions put to them, may lawfully find themselves the target of a prosecutorial attack.

Frank Schmalleger, *Criminal Justice Today*, p. 353

1. Circle the letter of the main idea.
   a. The rights of those who plead the Fifth Amendment have been upheld by the Supreme Court.
   b. Defendants who choose to testify in court can face hard questions by the prosecutors.
   c. The accused take the advice of their counsel as to whether they will testify.
2. Circle the statement that supports the main idea.
   a. TV shows and crime novels have made phrases such as "taking the Fifth" popular.
   b. The Fifth Amendment is a powerful ally of the criminal defendant.
   c. In the past, defendants who refused to testify were denigrated by the prosecutors.

A summary of supporting details, can also help in determining the main idea. Details, however, can be major or minor.

Major Details/Minor Details

Whether a particular detail is a major one depends on

a. The main point the writer is making, and
b. Whether the detail is essential in supporting, explaining, or changing the main idea in a significant way.

The following chart contrasts important differences between major and minor details.

Major Details	Minor Details
Directly support or explain the main idea	Often add information to a major detail
Are essential to the basic understanding of the paragraph or selection	Are not essential in developing a main idea—they simply help hold our attention and interest

When in doubt about whether a detail is major, first determine the main idea and then ask yourself these key questions:

Does the detail explain, support, or prove the main idea?
Does the detail add essential information or change the main idea in a major way?

For the following paragraph, determine the main idea and the major details. There may be more than one major detail.

The Reagan Revolution

Political change began in 1980, when Ronald Reagan rode the tide of American discontent to a narrow but decisively important victory in the presidential election. Building on a conservative critique of American policies and on issues that Jimmy Carter had placed on the national agenda, he presided over revolutionary changes in American government and policies. Reagan was a "Teflon president" who managed to take credit for successes but avoid blame for problems and rolled to a landslide reelection in 1984. The consequences of his two terms were startling. They included an altered role for government, powerful but selective economic growth, and a shift of domestic politics away from bread-and-butter issues toward moral or lifestyle concerns.

David Goldfield, et al., *The American Journey*

1. Write the main idea for this textbook passage.

   _____

   _____

2. Indicate whether each detail is major (MJ) or minor (MN).

   a. Political change began in 1980 _____

   b. Reagan built on conservative critique of Carter's policies _____

   c. Reagan presided over revolutionary changes in the government _____

   d. Reagan was a teflon president _____

   e. The consequences of his two terms were startling _____

   f. Domestic politics moved from bread and butter issues to moral concerns. _____

In the following chapter (4), you will learn how knowledge of organizational patterns can enhance your ability to locate the main idea and identify major and minor details.

CHAPTER 4

Recognizing Authors' Organizational Patterns

Textbook information is presented essentially in paragraph form. Most paragraphs contain sentences that are connected in meaning by some kind of pattern. To understand the paragraph, you have to see how the arrangement of the sentence parts fit together to shape the meaning. This *arrangement* is often referred to as an "organizational pattern."

Textbook authors *want* readers to understand the information presented so they organize text material in ways that makes learning easier. For this reason, they use thinking patterns with which we are all familiar. These patterns reflect the same ones we use when we think and speak to structure and organize our ideas. For example

Patterns of Speech/Thinking	An Example of the Pattern
Classifying and *enumerating* information or *dividing* it into parts	List class assignments.
Explaining the order in which something happened	Give directions.
Listing the steps in a process	Access computer information.
Giving *examples*	Discuss the kinds of exercises you do.
Comparing and *contrasting*	Decide whether to buy an American car or a foreign car.
Discussing a *cause* and its *effect*	Pass a course, because of diligent study.
Defining ideas or concepts	Explain your feelings about a career.

Although there are many ways to express ideas, writers usually use these seven basic patterns, generally mixing, overlapping, or combining them in paragraphs and passages. Therefore, the patterns can vary from page to page. When readers recognize the patterns, they are better able to process the information and think with the author. These patterns further help anticipate information, clarify topics or key ideas, and show the relationship of supporting statements.

The writer's purpose and the topic help determine the pattern or patterns to be used. Terms writers use to signal to the reader which pattern is being used should be familiar to you, since these are often the very words instructors use in exams and quizzes—for example, *define, compare, contrast, explain, list, describe, analyze*. You have probably encountered these words many times. Understanding writing patterns not only assists you in your reading/study tasks but also better prepares you to take examinations. These patterns can also serve as models or examples for your own writing tasks.

PATTERN 1: CLASSIFICATION

The classification pattern is used extensively by textbook authors. The pattern breaks information into parts or explains a series of things. Consequently, information is often placed into categories or classified by groups on the basis of similarities and/or differences. The reader needs to determine the *kinds* of categories and how they have been organized into specified groups. By means of this pattern, lengthy subject matter can be divided into many parts or "chunks," making it easier for the reader to remember.

The process used in classification often takes the form of an outline. The topic or main idea sentence usually helps identify the type of category. Writers often use numbers to signal a class or division, for example, *two classes*, or *three categories*, or *four divisions*.

Signal or guide words are an obvious clue for this pattern. Study those listed here so you will recognize them when you are reading and so you will be able to use them when you write answers on examinations and in your general writing.

Signals for Classification				
categories	features	sorts	characteristics	groups
types	classes	kinds	ways	classification
numbers	elements	parts		

Generally, a writer classifies information in a series of statements giving supporting facts or details. The order in which the information is presented is usually not significant and can be switched around without changing the meaning. Read the following paragraph to see whether the meaning would change if the second and third sentences were switched. The signal words are circled.

> The Chinese responded to prejudice and persecution in (two ways.) (First,) they created an insulated society-within-a-society that needed little from the dominant culture. (Second,) they displayed (a stoic) willingness to persevere, and to take without complaint or resistance whatever America dished out.
>
> Donald Dale Jackson, "Sojourners Who Came to Stay,"
> *Smithsonian*, Feb. 1991, p. 117

When studying textbook material, you may find it helpful to make some notations of the signal or guide words to assist you to understand information. Circling, highlighting, or underlining after an initial reading can help you recognize the parts of the classification. Then, outlining or mapping by creating a chart or diagram will simplify remembering the information when you study.

Read the following passage, marking the signal words as you do, and then study how it has been marked.

> Not all violence is the same. Various thinkers have categorized violence in several ways. One of the best is that of political scientist Fred R. van der Mehden, who sees five general types of violence.
>
> **PRIMORDIAL.** Primordial violence grows out of conflicts among the basic communities—ethnic, national, or religious— into which people are born. Rioting between Armenians and Azerbaizhanis in the Soviet Union, the multigroup war in Lebanon, and the tribal conflicts in some African nations are examples of primordial violence.
>
> **SEPARATIST.** Separatist violence, which is sometimes an outgrowth of primordial conflict, aims at independence for the group in question. The Ibos tried to break away from Nigeria with their new state of Biafra . . . but they were defeated in a

long and costly war . . . . In Europe, the Basques, Betons, and Corsicans have given rise to separatist movements.

REVOLUTIONARY. Revolutionary violence is aimed at overthrowing or replacing an existing regime. The Sandinistas' ouster of Somoza in Nicaragua in 1979, the fall of the Shah of Iran that same year, and the independence of the former Portuguese colonies of Angola and Mozambique in 1975 are examples of successful revolutionary violence. Central America and Southern Africa are scenes of continuing revolutionary violence . . . . The distinctive form of terror of our day, the car bomb, would probably come under the **rubric** of revolutionary violence as well.

COUPS. Coups are usually **counterrevolutionary** in intent, aimed at heading off a fear of revolutionary takeover. Coups are almost always military although the military usually has connections with and support from key civilian groups, as in the Brazilian coup of 1964. Most coups don't involve much violence at least initially. Army tanks surround the presidential palace, forcing the president's resignation and usually exile, and a general takes over as president. Some coups are virtually bloodless.

ISSUES. Some violence doesn't fit into any of these categories. Violence oriented to particular issues is a catchall category and generally less deadly than the other kind . . . the sometimes violent protests at nuclear power plants or missile sites, and the anger that grows around some economic problems are examples of issue-oriented violence.

All these categories—and others one might think of—are apt to be arbitrary. Some situations fit more than one category. Some start in one category and **escalate** into another. No country, even a highly developed one is totally immune to some kind of violence, however.

Michael G. Roskin, et al., *Political Science, An Introduction*

Study the significant markings from the previous passage dealing with violence. Answer the question that follows:

Not all violence is the same. <u>Various thinkers have categorized violence in</u> several ways. One of the best is that of political scientist Fred R. van der Mehden, who sees five general types of violence.

PRIMORDIAL. Primordial violence grows out of conflicts among the basic communities—ethnic, national, or religious—into which people are born.

SEPARATIST. Separatist violence, which is sometimes an outgrowth of primordial conflict, aims at independence for the group in question.

REVOLUTIONARY. Revolutionary violence is aimed at overthrowing or replacing an existing regime.

COUPS. Coups are usually **counterrevolutionary** in intent, aimed at heading off a fear of revolutionary takeover.

ISSUES. Some violence doesn't fit into any of these categories. Violence oriented to particular issues is a catchall category and generally less deadly than the other kind . . . the sometimes violent protests at nuclear power plants or missile sites, and the anger that grows around some economic problems are examples of issue-oriented violence.

What type of violence would we most likely find in the United States?

_____

_____

PATTERN 2: SEQUENCE (3 TYPES)

1. *Time Order/Chronology*: Paragraph or passage details are usually presented in the order in which they happen.

   Example: Text information shows how a Congressional bill becomes a law.

2. *Spatial Order*: Paragraph or passage details are organized in order of their occurrence.

   Example: Steps that must be followed in order in a chemical experiment.

3. *Place Order*: Paragraph or passage details are placed so that they are understood in terms of their relative position.

   Example: The location of the particular stars in a galaxy.

Unlike the order in the classification pattern, the order in sequence is significant and cannot be changed. For example, a history book can use time order to explain a series of events in a war, while a biology text can use a time sequence to show the evolutionary stages of animals. A manual on automotive transmissions can explain repairs in their order of importance, in a sequence of steps.

Generally, signal words help the reader see which important details will be developed in a sequential pattern. As with the classification pattern, numbers may be used, but for the purpose of showing time order or steps in a process, not for the purpose of merely listing at random. The major signal words to help you recognize the sequence pattern follow.

Signals for Sequence		
first	now	later
second	after	stages
third	before	steps
next	finally	then
most important	furthermore	when
last		

As you read the following paragraph written in one of the sequence patterns, draw a circle around the signal words; this will help you follow and remember the order.

The author of Roe [vs. Wade], Justice Harry Blackmun, set down the following rules for abortion in the 7–2 majority opinion: During the first three months of pregnancy, the decision to end the pregnancy is left to the woman and her doctor. During the second trimester, states may regulate the circumstances under which abortion is performed in order to protect the health of the woman. In the final three months, when the fetus is presumed able to survive outside the womb, states are permitted to forbid abortion except to preserve the life or health of the mother.

The ink was hardly dry on the court's order when efforts to counter it began.

"Beyond the Rhetoric" SIRS

Did you circle first, second, and final three

PATTERN 3: SIMPLE LISTING

There is a significant difference between using the patterns of classification and sequence and simply listing details.

> In the classification pattern, numbers are used to designate various components—*two ways, three kinds,* and so on. The components are presented in random order.
>
> In the sequence pattern, numbers are used to indicate a *particular* order and are not random: *the first step, the second step.*
>
> In the simple listing pattern, writers develop their ideas by *listing* their supporting statements. They simply list or enumerate a series of details that support a point. The details may be examples, reasons, or types of things, and they are often, *but not always,* numbered.
>
> This pattern is used where there are several important points the author wants to present; however, the order in which the lists are arranged is not important. What the reader must do is see how the items in the list are related to each other. For example, an author might list the four main functions of e-mail but not necessarily develop or expand them.

Signals for Simple Listing	
1, 2, 3, 4	another
a, b, c, d	moreover
first, second	next
also	then

Notice the random order of the following western civilization choices for text inclusion on drug problems in the workplace.

> Although I have not found a central thread from which to hang the selections in this book, I have not chosen them arbitrarily. Instead, I have adopted three general criteria to guide my selection of documents: (1) That the document be of major significance, shaping the history of an important society or succession of societies through time; (2) that the document give us substantial insights into the nature of the society from which it sprang,

either at a given period of its history or over a long period of time; and (3) that the document be intrinsically interesting. Almost all of the selections in this book satisfy one.

Oliver Johnson, *Sources of World Civilization*

PATTERN 4: EXAMPLE

The example pattern is one of the most common writing patterns and fairly easy to recognize. Often, one or more examples or illustrations will be used to support a main idea or explain or clarify a concept. Good examples help to make general ideas more specific and also aid in holding the reader's interest. The following signal words often identify this pattern:

Signals for Example		
for example	to illustrate	such as
for instance	specifically	

Read the following passages to see how each author gave numerous examples to develop the main point. If you first determine the main idea, you will readily see how examples are used to illustrate or clarify the important information. In textbook reading, examples are rarely the main point; rather, they support the major ideas.

The Church not only opposed all non-Christian faiths it encountered in Europe, it also condemned all pagan beliefs and rituals retained by its converts, a not uncommon phenomenon. In 743 the Synod of Rome outlawed offerings to pagan deities, and in 744 the Council of Leptinnes drew up an extensive "List of Superstitions," which it prohibited. The council approved a baptismal formula wherein the catechumen renounced all "works of the demon, and all his words," to wit it mentioned Thor, Odin, and other northern European pagan deities. In 829 the Synod of Paris reasoned that since the Bible (see Exodus 22:18) decreed that they should not be permitted to live, kings should have the right to punish sorcerers severely. And, indeed, kings did assume such powers, even executing sorcerers where their incantations resulted in death.[11]

Bryan LeBeau, *The Story of the Salem Witch Trials*

Underline two examples that support the main idea.

The quest to improve American life went far beyond protest movements, but it showed the same energy, the same intensity that Stanton or the crusaders brought to their lives. It might be seen in the Chautauqua movement. Meeting in the countryside, seated in tents or on the rude wooden benches of amphitheaters, millions of men and women gathered yearly to hear public readings, illustrated lectures, organ recitals, and scientific demonstrations.[26] Across the North, the improving instinct showed itself in the village-improvement societies that women created, to salvage what little of nature the towns still had. The spirit could stir itself in matters as small as the spring day that the ladies of Guilford, Connecticut, set aside for raking the village green—as expansive as the Catholic utopian women's community that Martha White McWhirter founded in Texas—as broad and far-reaching as the movement to create women's colleges with standards as rigorous as those for men: Vassar in 1865, Smith, Wellesley, Mills, Bryn Mawr, and then, as adjuncts to universities exclusively male, Radcliffe and Barnard.[27]

Mark Summers, *The Gilded Age*

Underline two examples that support the main idea.

Pattern 5: Comparison and Contrast

In comparing ideas or things, writers explain similarities between them; in contrasting ideas or things, writers show differences. Writers often use the comparison-and-contrast method to show the positive and negative sides, or advantages and disadvantages of an issue or event. Frequently, writers may make comparisons and contrasts within the same passage. Listing similarities or differences in a column format is a good note making device as it helps the reader sort out and remember major points.

Readers can readily spot this pattern because of the words used to signal likenesses and differences:

Signals for Comparison		
compare	like/alike	resembles
in comparison	likewise	similar
in the same way/manner	parallels	similarly
Signals for Contrast		
although	different	on the contrary
as opposed to	however	on the other hand
but	in contrast to	rather than
conversely	instead	unlike
difference	nevertheless	whereas
		yet

Does the following passage compare, contrast, or compare-and-contrast two characteristics?

At the purely personal level, the religious experiences of all three traditions, Mesopotamian, Egyptian, and Israelite, seem at times to be almost interchangeable. The anguish of Job in biblical literature has its counterpart in the Babylonian Ludlul bel Nemeqi. Some of the psalms, and the wisdom literature in general (Proverbs, Ecclesiastes, Sirach, for example), share a common outlook, content, and sometimes even verbal similarities with the religious literature of the other traditions. The presence in the Bible of a love lyric, the Song of Songs, reveals the extraordinarily diverse religious background of which the Bible is itself a diverse reflection. The monotheism (or henotheism) of the pharaoh Akh-en-aton seems to have been a form of personal religion that he tried (unsuccessfully) to extend to all of Egypt, whereas that of Israel was the product of the historical experience of the nation as a whole.

Brendan Nagle, *The Ancient World:*
Readings in Social and Cultural History

Pattern 6: Cause-and-Effect Relationship

When writers present arguments or describe events, one of the most frequently used patterns is cause and effect. The writer discusses *why* or *how* something happened and *what* the results are or might be. The cause is the *reason* or *motive*; the effect is the *result, consequence,* or *outcome.*

This pattern is used extensively in scientific and technical textbooks. It is also one of the chief techniques of reasoning and, therefore, a common pattern found in persuasive and argumentative writing. Cause and effect can be used in various combinations to express a paragraph's main idea.

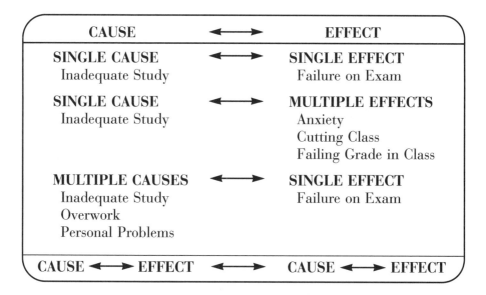

CAUSE	⟷	EFFECT
SINGLE CAUSE Inadequate Study	⟷	**SINGLE EFFECT** Failure on Exam
SINGLE CAUSE Inadequate Study	⟷	**MULTIPLE EFFECTS** Anxiety Cutting Class Failing Grade in Class
MULTIPLE CAUSES Inadequate Study Overwork Personal Problems	⟷	**SINGLE EFFECT** Failure on Exam

CAUSE ⟷ EFFECT   ⟷   CAUSE ⟷ EFFECT

Signals for Cause		
because	due to	on account of
cause	for this reason	since
		why
Signals for Effect		
as a result	in effect	therefore
consequently	result	thus
hence	the outcome is	

Notice the various key words that signal a series of cause-and-effect relationships in the following paragraph.

> The same concern for centralizing control within the White House affected the conduct of foreign relations. Nixon and Henry Kissinger, his national security adviser, saw the official foreign-policy agencies—including the departments of State and Defense and the CIA—as often uninformed and as consistently unimaginative. Worse, Nixon and Kissinger believed, these branches of government were filled with individuals who would obstruct presidential initiatives or, as in the case of Daniel Ellsberg, leak sensitive and secret material to the press. As a result of their fears and their desire for greater White House power, Nixon and Kissinger began to conduct their own secret foreign policy—secret from the American people and from other government officials as well. Their decision in 1970 to begin heavy bombing of neutral Cambodia, for example, deliberately bypassed high officials in the State and Defense departments.

Pattern 7: **Definition**

In the definition pattern, the author's purpose is to explain the meaning of an important term or concept; it can take an entire paragraph to do so. In all academic subjects, some key terms and concepts are crucial to your understanding the text and subject matter.

Sometimes a title, a subtitle, or the first sentence of a paragraph, appearing in question form, indicates that the definition pattern will be used. Often, other writing patterns are incorporated into a passage where a definition is being presented.

In textbook writing, definitions tend to be **straightforward**, as in scientific textbooks. In other situations, authors use the definition pattern to explain technical language, important terminology, and concepts. **Abstract** terms, such as those used in sociology and philosophy, are less precise in meaning, however, and may require more lengthy explanations. The following paragraph demonstrates how even a simple term like *the Age of Enlightenment* has its own special meaning in a contemporary textbook.

> Educated colonists were especially interested in the new ideas that characterized what has been called the **Age of Enlightenment**. The European thinkers of the Enlightenment drew inspiration from recent advances in science—such as the English scientist

Isaac Newton's explanation of the laws of gravity—that suggested that the universe operated according to natural laws that human reason could discover. They also drew on the work of the English philosopher John Locke, who maintained that God did not dictate human knowledge but rather gave us the power to acquire knowledge through experience and understanding. The hallmark of Enlightenment thought was thus a belief in the power of human reason to improve the human condition.

David Goldfield et al., *The American Journey*

This definition can be mapped as follows.

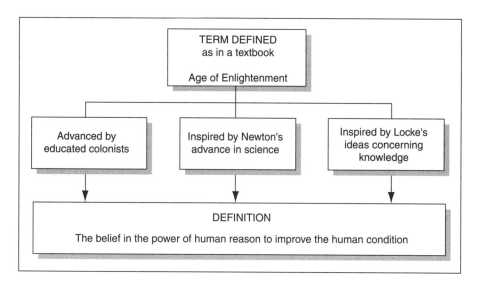

One way to recognize the writer's pattern is through signal or clue words. Signal words most commonly used to indicate the definition pattern include the following:

Signals for Definition		
define	known as	we mean
is	that is, i.e.	we can state
is defined as	the term means	

Writers can employ the seven organizational patterns separately or in combination. Be aware of the signal words so you can recognize them both in reading and in examinations. You need to realize, however, that signal words, like the patterns themselves, can overlap. This is the case with classification and sequence, which both use numbers (1, 2, 3; first, second, third). Also, numbers are used frequently when a writer wants to present a *list* of items.

In the following chapter, we will begin to examine critical reading and thinking in more detail.

CHAPTER 5

Critical Thinking Skills

The main purpose in reading textbooks is to increase knowledge by learning new information. However, just as important, readers must also evaluate the information and ideas suggested or merely hinted at by the author. Thinking beyond the basic facts and information and gaining additional insights into what the author has presented is what critical reading is all about. It is in the thinking process itself that information becomes our own and is retained.

The elements of thinking critically in textbook reading include

making valid inferences by
> separating facts from opinions
> evaluating the main ideas and supporting details and
> drawing logical conclusions
recognizing an author's attitude and point of view
distinguishing denotative and connotative language
understanding the author's tone and purpose

When reading critically, you often will need to reread and rethink what you have studied.

MAKING INFERENCES: DAILY DETECTIVE WORK

One important aspect of critical comprehension involves making inferences while you read. *Making an inference means forming your own conclusion by reasoning on the basis of what has been suggested by a writer but not stated directly.*

Inference, as it applies to reading, may be new to you, but we all make inferences daily using our intuition and feelings. We draw inferences from people's facial expressions, tone of voice, or body language. For instance, if your boss scowls at you when you arrive late for work, you can infer that she is unhappy with your tardiness. You make an "educated," reasonable guess based on limited information, weighing known facts in light of your background knowledge and past experience. Making inferences is reasoning out what you see, or what you read.

To be a critical reader, you need to make connections between what the writer says *and* what the writer wants you to understand. When you are trying to interpret a writer's views on a topic, especially if the issue is political, economic, or social, your own cultural background and assumptions play a major role as you reason, make inferences, and draw conclusions. To increase your inferential thinking in reading textbook material, it is important to ask questions as you read.

LOGICAL REASONING LEADS TO VALID INFERENCES AND SOUND CONCLUSIONS

A *valid* inference is a conclusion or generalization based on clear evidence and logical reasoning about that evidence. An *invalid* inference is an assumption that is supported by inadequate evidence or arrived at through faulty logic. For example,

> Most Americans get their political information from television and most say they believe information obtained from television more than that in newspapers.

> Michael G. Roskin, et al. *Political Science*

Possible valid inferences from this statement might be

1. Television is shaping America's political views more than newspapers.
2. Most Americans place less value on newspaper reporting than on television news.

Each of these inferences could be made from the statement. An inference, then, is not a statement that appears in print on the page but rather is formed through reasoning with what is given but not stated directly. In the example, the author suggests the popularity of television news over the newspaper, but none of the inferential statements are specifically expressed; they result from logically interpreting the textbook statement.

The following inferential statements would both be *invalid*:

1. It would be cheaper for Americans to buy a daily newspaper than a television set for getting the news.

2. The American public is illiterate and relies on television for information.

There is nothing in the textbook statement about cost or literacy. Usually, an invalid inference results either when a reader's thinking goes beyond what the writer has implied or when the reader's conclusion comes from his or her *own* preconceived ideas. We make sense of our world by thinking, and inferential thinking is actually reasoning and drawing conclusions from what is indirectly stated. In effect, inferential thinking is "detective thinking."

Critical readers try to uncover "hidden" or indirectly stated meanings, when they exist in much the way a detective looks for clues and evidence. When a writer suggests an idea indirectly, it is called an *implication*. The reader's inferences are attempts to understand a writer's implications. A reader *infers*; a writer *implies*. Some people refer to inference as "reading between the lines."

Reading between the Lines

Why do writers sometimes "hide" their ideas and imply them rather than express them directly? They do so for several reasons:

1. To encourage readers to do their own thinking and draw their own conclusions.
2. To conceal an unpopular notion, a biased opinion, or a persuasive appeal.
3. To manipulate the unsuspecting reader.

STRATEGIES FOR MAKING VALID INFERENCES

Use the following strategies when making valid inferences and drawing sound conclusions.

Strategy 1: Separate the facts from the opinions.
Strategy 2: Evaluate the main ideas and supporting details.
Strategy 3: Test the logic of your inferences.

Let's begin looking at the first strategy.

Strategy 1: Separating the Facts from the Opinions

Much of what you read is designed to influence your thinking. The critical reader judges which statements to accept and which to question further by first distinguishing facts from opinions. It is not always easy to recognize whether a statement is a fact, an opinion, or a combination of both. Writers are influenced by their own opinions as they write and interpret information. Moreover, as they try to persuade you to their way of thinking, they sometimes word their opinions to appear as facts.

Additionally, your own opinions can influence you when you are evaluating persuasive writing. You may tend to respond positively to ideas that confirm your own beliefs or deny ideas contrary to your belief system. In fairness to the writer, you need to be open-minded while weighing the merits of arguments; but, at the same time, you must always examine ideas carefully so you do not accept everything in print to be truthful. When evaluating what you read, ask yourself

Is the author right about this?

Are there enough facts and valid arguments, or are the statements simply opinions?

Can the author's idea be proved?

Can the ideas be supported?

Facts

What exactly is a fact, and how can a fact be distinguished from an opinion? *A statement of fact is one that can definitely be verified or proved or tested by experiment.* Facts can be verified, for example, in official documents, reference books, and legal records. They contain information based on some kind of direct evidence, experience, or observation. Facts are not only used to support main points and concepts but often are used to support other facts.

All of the following statements are facts, and each can be verified.

At Sagres in 1419 Prince Henry established a center to develop ships and maps that enabled Portugal to extend its sway down the coast of western Africa.

By the time the Church was legalized in A.D. 313, the life of the historical Jesus was three centuries in the past.

As a critical reader, you should evaluate statements of fact to determine whether they are current, relevant, and representative. A statement of fact may be true or false, since facts about the world change as scientists and scholars discover more information and gain new insights.

Opinions

A statement of opinion cannot be proved true or false. It may not necessarily be incorrect; it just has not been proved and cannot be objectively verified. Statements of opinion usually express personal beliefs, feelings, attitudes, values, interpretations, or judgments that someone has about a subject or topic. Opinions are often based on inferences, hunches, guesses, or conclusions.

The following statements are opinions:

> As both a challenger and an incumbent, Reagan primarily ran as Ronald Reagan and only secondarily as a Republican with a coherent philosophy and concrete program.

(More so than other candidates? Would all Republicans agree?)

> In many areas, Nixon's record did look bad.

(Did it look good in others? Bad for whom?)

Although opinions cannot be checked for accuracy, writers need to support or back their opinions with evidence, facts, and reasons before they can convince readers. You need to determine whether stated opinions are reasonable, based on available information.

An Informed Opinion

Although an opinion cannot be proven as a fact can, an opinion can be supported with evidence from the author's research. This is known as an *informed opinion*. Most writing contains statements that combine both facts and opinion. A critical reader knows when the fact(s) end and the opinion begins in any given statement.

Word Watch

The critical reader notices words that signal opinions rather than facts.

I believe	I suggest	She alleged	It apparently is
I conclude	I surmise	He appeared to	It seems that
I feel/think	I hold that	They usually	It probably will

A note of caution: Do not be misled into accepting statements as facts simply because they have been prefaced with any of the following expressions:

As a matter of fact	The fact of the matter is
In fact	The point is
It is a fact that	The truth is

Many times these words or phrases are followed by an opinion, as in the following statement: "The point is that not everyone should learn a foreign language." There is no fact in the statement, and whether everyone *should* learn a foreign language or not is one person's opinion.

Review the difference between a statement of fact and opinion by studying the following map before completing the next practice activity.

Judge whether the following statements are facts (F), opinions (O), or combinations of both (F/O). If a statement is a direct quotation, do not consider it a fact simply because someone has said it. The person making the statement may be merely expressing his or her opinion.

If a statement contains an opinion, indicate whether you can accept what is said because it reveals an informed, not a personal, opinion.

_____ **1.** Most ethnographers agree that the Pueblo were a sexually spirited people.

> John Mack Faragher et al, *Out of Many: A History of the American People*

_____ **2.** Archaeological evidence to date reveals an urban civilization with its roots beginning as early as 7000 B.C.E. in simple settlements like Mehrgarh in the foothills of the Bolan Pass.

> Howard Spodek, *The World's History*

_____ **3.** World War II, far more than World War I, deserves to be called a global conflict.

> Michael J. Lyons, *World War II: A Short History*

_____

_____

_____ **4.** Few modern scholars believe the Reconstruction governments established in the South in 1867 and 1868 fulfilled the aspirations of their humble constituents.

> Eric Foner, "The New View of Reconsturction,"rpt in John R. M. Wilson., *Forging the American Character, Volume I: Readings in United States History to 1877.*

_____

_____

_____ **5.** Authorities differ widely on the location of these three lands, but the most widely accepted theory is that they are Baffin Island, Labrador, and Newfoundland--all of which are only a few hundred miles from Greenland.

> Jerome R. Reich, *Colonial America*

_____

_____

Strategy 2: Evaluating the Main Idea and Supporting Details

Making inferences from the main ideas and supporting details is somewhat similar to making inferences from facts. You need also, however, to pay particular attention to the sequence of thought in support of the views expressed. To guide yourself in following the sequence, make marginal notations of the most important ideas, such as those you make in locating the main idea, and then evaluate these notations.

In the following passage on our competitive society, marginal notations have been made to assist you in making valid inferences. Also, important qualifying terms have been circled.

Population of Europeans in North America increased in seventeenth century.

At the beginning of the seventeenth century the European presence north of Mexico was extremely limited; two Spanish bases in Florida, a few Franciscan missionaries among the Pubelos, and fishermen along the North Atlantic coast. By 1700 the human landscape of the Southwest, the South and the Northeast had been transformed. More than a quarter million Europeans and Africans had moved into these three regions, the vast majority to the British colonies. Indian societies had been disrupted, depopulated, and in some cases destroyed.

Increased European presence had disastrous results for Indian societies.

John Mack Faragher et al, *Out of Many: A History of the American People*

One can infer from the paragraph that the increased settlement of the North America by Europeans led to the decreased population of its native inhabitants. This is supported by the author's statements that "By 1700," when "more than a quarter million Europeans and Africans" had settled into regions of North America, "Indian societies had been disrupted, depopulated, and in some cases destroyed."

Notice that it becomes easier to make inferences once you understand the stated ideas and have examined the particular supporting details that develop these ideas.

Be Aware of Signal Words That Qualify the Meaning of the Main Idea and Major Details

As you recall from your study of fact and opinion, you need to be aware of words that qualify meanings. The chart following group the major signal words into four categories according to how they qualify a statement or what they imply about the author's attitude toward his or her statements.

Signal Words That Qualify Meaning

Signal Words of Inference

The following words may signal an implication *by the writer*. Recall that the writer implies, and the reader infers.

assumption	it is assumed; one can assume; the assumption is
implication	this implies; it may be implied; the result implies
inference	one can infer; this may infer; the inference is
suggestion	this may suggest; it could be suggested; the suggestion here is

Absolute Signal Words

These words should make the reader reject a statement unless there is strong support.

always	definitely	irrefutably
assuredly	indisputably	undeniably
certainly	invariably	without question

Probability Signal Words

These words suggest that the information may be accurate but that other possibilities may exist.

almost	probably
presumably	there is little question

Possibility Signal Words

These words suggest that the ideas are subject to debate and that there is doubt as to their complete validity.

apparently	perhaps
could be	possibly
likely	seems
may/maybe	seemingly
might	somewhat

Strategy 3: Assessing the Logic of Your Inferences and Sound Conclusions

You can assess the logic of your inferences by making a check mark in the margin by the evidence that supports it. If you can find no support, the inference is probably unreliable. The more support presented for the inference, the more likely it is to be valid.

Use two key questions to help you judge the logic of your inferences.

- What support validates my inference?

Ask: Is this what has been suggested? Can this inference be justified?

- Is my inference a valid one?

Ask: Does it make sense? Is it reasonable based on the facts? Is the development of ideas logical?

Use these same key questions when drawing conclusions from inferences you have made, substituting the word *conclusion*.

- What support has the author provided for the conclusion I have drawn?
- Is my conclusion valid?

When you infer the implications an author makes, you are drawing a conclusion. Drawing your *own* conclusion based on valid inferences is an important aspect of critical reading since much of what we read consists of assumptions made by the writers. An assumption is the author's opinion that he or she believes to be true.

When an author writes statements such as the following, they are an assumptions—opinions the author believes to be true.

> George Bush, Reagan's vice president and successor as president, loved to run the world by Rolodex and telephone. When someone's name came up at a formal dinner, he was likely to grab a phone and ring the person up. He upgraded the hot line to Moscow from a teletype machine to a modern communications system. When Congress was heading in the wrong direction, he started dialing senators and representatives. When a crisis threatened world peace, he had the same reaction—pick up the phone and start chatting with presidents and prime ministers. He viewed diplomacy as a series of conversations and friendships among leaders, not the reconciliation of differing national interests.
>
> David Goldfield, et al., *The American Journey*

In contrast, when *you* make a judgment, *you* evaluate whether a statement deserves support or has merit in a particular situation.

> For example, were all crises handled by telephone? Is this bad? Did Bush ever negotiate in person? Did he never consider the national interest?

Therefore, judgments are reasonable evaluations of particular ideas, concepts, and situations.

As you read, engage in a dialogue with the author, questioning whether the author is correct about his or her beliefs. At the same time, be open-minded to new ideas that may challenge those you hold. Remember that your own experience and what you know about a topic may sometimes be limited, and you may have to reevaluate some of your previously held ideas.

The following chart lists steps in arriving at valid inferences, sound conclusions, and unbiased judgments.

Making Valid Inferences, Drawing Sound Conclusions, and Forming Unbiased Judgments

UNDERSTAND THE ISSUE AND PROBLEM.	Identify the thesis and supporting evidence.
SEPARATE THE FACTS FROM OPINIONS.	Verify the facts. Note whether the opinions are informed or simply the author's assumptions.
BEWARE OF BIAS.	Identify the author's bias or biases concerning the issue. Identify your own bias or biases concerning the issue.
USE YOUR EXPERIENCE.	Look to your own experience, but evaluate how limited it might be in regard to the issue.
REASON AND THINK ABOUT THE ISSUE.	Identify fallacies in the writer's arguments. Identify fallacies in your *own* reasoning.
BECOME A CRITICAL READER.	Make valid inferences. Draw sound conclusions. Form unbiased judgments.

THE AUTHOR'S POINT OF VIEW

Textbook writing often reflects the author's *point of view* toward a subject. This attitude, based on the writer's beliefs, helps the writer decide what is important to include and/or exclude, and, also, how much emphasis to place on certain information. For example, when an author gives a very detailed explanation for the causes of the Civil War, it should suggest to the critical reader that the author thinks this problem is extremely important.

In general terms, point of view tells the reader "where the author is coming from." It is in effect the writer's particular *bias*, the angle from which he or she views things—the position or stance the writer takes. Both readers and writers have biases, preconceived ideas or judgments.

It is only natural that a person's background would influence his or her views or opinions on a particular topic. For example, would not an article written on alcoholism have a different perspective if influenced by an interview with a member of Alcoholics Anonymous? A doctor? A priest? You should therefore examine the writer's point of view so as to recognize what bias of prejudice the writer expresses. The critical reader asks these key questions.

1. Is the writer's position for or against an issue? What does this imply about the writer?
2. How do the biases and beliefs of the author affect the presentation of ideas?

When subject matter presented is controversial in nature, the critical reader must determine which side the writer favors. If the writer presents only one side of an issue, the writing is generally *subjective* or opinionated and often biased. If all sides of an issue are presented, the writing may be neutral and *objective* or impartial. Subjective writing that reflects the author's viewpoint does not necessarily make it "bad" or something to be rejected immediately. The terms "neutral" and "objective" may make it seem that the writer is completely fair, honest and impartial, and the words "subjective" and "biased" may make the author's information sound unfair and one-sided, but this may not be so. Do not think that only objective writing should be accepted, or that all biased writing should be rejected.

Critical readers think seriously about what has been presented, particularly new ideas that may challenge their already preconceived beliefs. The *critical reading* of textbook material, therefore, can help readers reshape their own point of view toward an issue and can play a significant role in modifying their thinking. What the reader needs to do is evaluate the ideas to see if the author's point of view differs from the reader's own and what to accept, reject, or modify.

Why is it important to recognize the author's point of view in a textbook? Because it helps the reader understand how the author, in accumulating the information for the textbook, has *interpreted* the recorded concepts and theories as well as facts. To illustrate, even experts who write on the same subject may disagree or emphasize differently the significance of things. An examination of two textbooks that deal with the causes of the Civil War would show differences in the degree of emphasis and the point of view.

For example, would not a chapter written on the causes of the Civil War have a different perspective if influenced by Southern or Northern accounts? Political or economic accounts? Soldiers or slave accounts?

The ability to search out and understand differing perspectives is *the cornerstone of critical thinking and reading.* As a critical reader, you need to understand the point of view of others, questioning the facts, opinions, and ideas expressed, as you analyze the writer's point of view. Critical readers should think and then ask themselves whether the author changed their minds or at least exposed them to new or different positions.

As indicated earlier, authors do not always state their stance or position directly. The reader may have to carefully combine what authors say directly with the clues they provide through word choices that infer their position. In making these analyses, the critical reader raises questions:

Is the support one-sided or objective?
Are the sources quoted and the references indicated sufficient and reliable?
Does the writer have the necessary background to write on the subject?
Are the word choices chosen objectively descriptive?

Read the following differing points of view of particular people in connection with the Constitution. Note the descriptions of the authors at the time they made the statements, and then answer the questions that follow.

T. Boone Pickens, a Texas millionaire

Through my experience with free enterprise, my appreciation continues to grow from the Constitution's principles of limited government and the freedom of individuals to achieve their maximum potential.

Ralph Nader, a consumer advocate

There should be a constitutional amendment that forbids a corporation from being treated as a person. You can't have equal protection of the laws when an individual is contesting against an Exxon.

Bernie Sanders, socialist mayor of Burlington, Vermont

The most obvious weakness of our Constitution is that the economic rights of our citizens are not adequately addressed. Freedom must mean more than the right to vote every four years for a candidate for President. Freedom must also mean the right of a citizen to decent income, decent shelter, decent health care, decent educational opportunity and decent retirement benefits. One is not free sleeping out in the streets. One is not free eating cat food in order to survive.

Excerpted from "Contention and Continuity," *Time*,
July 6, 1987, pp. 56–57

1. How do the three views differ? What are the particular biases of each?

DISTINGUISHING THE TWO DIMENSIONS OF LANGUAGE

As you have just learned, word choice is often an indication of the writer's attitude toward the subject. Awareness of the language the writer uses is both essential for making valid inferences and for recognizing the author's point of view. Language, however, has two dimensions. When reading, therefore, you will need to recognize both the *denotation* and *connotation* of words.

> *Denotation refers to a word's literal meaning, its accepted dictionary definition.*
> *Denotation is the meaning of a word independent of any emotional association.*

Textbook writers most often use denotative language to state facts as in the following example:

Processing of agricultural products was one of the major businesses in the late nineteenth century. Into the 1880s, flour milling was the leading industry, ranking ahead of lumbering. Meanwhile, the manufacturing of products from cottonseed steadily increased in importance, ranking second in the state's industrial economy in 1900. Meat packing, which began at Victoria in 1868, was soon extended to other communities, and a number of small plants added to the output. A small packing plant was built in Fort Worth in 1884; six years later, the Fort Worth stockyards were opened; and thereafter the packing business in that city expanded rapidly. Textile manufacturing began before the Civil War when a frontier businessman set up a cotton mill in New Braunfels. A plant manufacturing cotton goods was operated in the penitentiary for a number of years during and after the Civil War. Later, plants were established in Dallas, Sherman, and Post, but they remained comparatively unimportant.

Rupert Richardson et. al., *Texas: The Lone Star State*

It is not enough to know the dictionary definition of words; you must also understand their suggested meaning to avoid manipulation by writers with a particular bias. When the meaning of a word goes beyond its accepted, agreed-upon dictionary definition, it becomes the *connotation* of the word.

Connotation includes all the ideas, associations, and implications suggested above and beyond the dictionary definition.

Connotations may be either positive or negative. Depending on how they are used, many words can produce an emotional response in the reader, stir up the reader's feelings or create a visual image. Some words, however, are stronger in connotation than others. For example, the word *jail* generally suggests a dreary somber place where one is forced to spend time while *correctional facility* suggests a place of healing. A clear example of how the connotation of words can be shifted in emphasis is found in the famous remark of Bertrand Russell, the philosopher and author, "I am *firm*; you are *stubborn*; he is *pig-headed*." While all three terms have a similar denotative meaning, their connotations are obviously quite different.

A textbook writer has many options in choosing particular words. Writers realize their ability to make you react emotionally and arouse a particular response. For example, textbook authors imply approval of their ideas by using words with positive connotations, words that flatter or even exaggerate, such as *excellent, superb,* and *outstanding.* While these words imply approval, negative words that criticize—*grossly unfair, awkward,* and *ignorant*—imply disapproval.

Ask this key question to evaluate writers' attempts to influence your thinking by the importance or slant of their words.

Are the descriptive words used primarily positive or negative, favorable or unfavorable, pleasant or unpleasant?

Once you have identified the connotative language used, you can more accurately understand an author's attitude toward the subject. In order to distinguish positive or negative connotations and the writer's slant, it is helpful to underline, circle, or highlight those words. By the end of the reading, you will have a visual record of the essential words used and can more readily infer how the writer feels about the subject. Read the following passage. After noting the words, decide whether they are chiefly positive or negative. Then, answer the question that follows:

A Gilded Age

How far apart the images of the late nineteenth-century America stand! On one side, the Gilded Age shines as an era not of novelty but of charming antiquity: high-button shoes and gingerbread houses, and boys squirming in the dresses and tresses that *Little Lord Fauntleroy* made fashionable. In this fabulous world of wistful memory, gay '90s gentlemen sporting waxed mustaches tip their derbies at overdressed, overfed ladies on a stroll through the park and every ride down the boulevards takes place on bicycles built for two. One might almost imagine that unkempt customers looking for a shave in lather drubbed up out of their own personalized mugs faced no hazard worse in life than a barbershop quartet interrupting the strokes of the straight razor with "She's Only a Bird in a Gilded Cage."

Historians think they know better. For them, the era has earned the name that it first received in 1873, with the appearance of a best-selling novel by Charles Dudley Warner and Mark Twain, satirizing the way the pursuit of the almighty dollar fostered political corruption and speculative manias: *The Guilded Age.* Beneath the thinnest of gold coatings lay a leaden world, where everything was judged by its price in the market. Greed, graft, poverty, misery, upheaval, and bigotry stained the age indelibly. An image sticks in the mind of material accomplishment and spiritual paucity. It is reflected in a traveler's description of the railroad line across the Missouri River into Omaha. "This bridge is of an immense length," he wrote. "The bed of the river was quite dry."[1]

Mark Summers, *The Gilded Age*

What do the descriptive words suggest?

_____

_____

TUNING IN TO TONE

When people speak, we generally recognize their attitude, feelings, or point of view by their tone of voice and physical gestures. In writing, the tone is chiefly controlled by the words the writer chooses, words that color ideas, evoke desired emotions, and imply judgments. Recognizing a writer's tone is a valuable clue to determine purpose (*why* the writer says something) and point of view (*how* the writer looks at a topic), both important in critical reading.

Tone is the manner in which writers express themselves and convey their feelings. It is the emotional message behind their words, reflecting their attitude toward the subject matter. "An important function of language," says Richard Altick in his *Preface to Critical Reading*, "is to mold the reader's attitude towards the subject discussed. Tone determines just what that attitude should be."

Depending on the purpose, an author's tone will vary. For example, if the purpose is to entertain, a humorous tone might be used. If the purpose is to voice disapproval, a sarcastic, bitter tone is displayed. When writing seriously, an author generally uses a serious tone.

To determine the author's tone, a critical reader can ask these two key questions.

1. How does the writer use words?
2. What is the writer's attitude?

Authors use a variety of tones in writing as listed below:

accusing	dignified	incredulous	outspoken
authoritative	distressed	insulting	pessimistic
caustic	evasive	irreverent	righteous
comical	fervent	mocking	scornful

Textbook writers, however, generally use the following tones, briefly described:

Serious or neutral tone: This tone is used in writing that focuses on important topics and is presented in a straightforward manner. The term *neutral* is sometimes used to indicate the author is being objective in presenting both sides of an issue.

Critical tone: The writer expresses judgments on what is good or bad about something. When criticizing, the writer may directly state approval or disapproval.

Cynical tone: The writer is not only negatively critical but also expresses doubt about the goodness of human actions or motives. Words used are often angry and pessimistic. The author's attitude is that humankind is selfish and corrupt and always acts out of self-interest.

Sarcastic tone: Like cynicism, sarcasm too is negatively critical and, here, words used are often harsh and bitter. While cynicism tries to show that people are selfish, sarcasm tries to show that people are foolish.

Humorous and witty tone: A humorous tone, intended to create laughter and entertain or amuse, can point out the foolishness or stupidity of humankind in a gentle way. When humor is used with irony or sarcasm, however, its intention usually is to ridicule.

Writing that expresses humor that is sophisticated is said to be witty. For example, when author Dorothy Parker was informed that President Coolidge, an extremely quiet and reserved man, had died, she remarked, "How can they tell?" A witty tone is often clever and thought-provoking, while a humorous tone is simply enjoyable.

UNDERSTANDING THE AUTHOR'S PURPOSE

Tone and purpose are closely related. A writer's purpose becomes apparent once you examine the words and determine their tone.

At times, writers want to influence you, *to persuade* you. Often, they write to help you learn: *to inform* you. They may wish to describe a place or event: *narrate* to you. Or, they may try to amuse you: *to entertain* you. But they can also combine their purposes. Entertaining writing can be used to persuade, for example. In textbook writing, when the main purpose is to provide information, the writer can shift from facts, *informing* you, to a personal anecdote or story to *amuse* you.

Since a writer does not usually say, "In this chapter, I intend to entertain you or prove to you or argue that . . . ," it is up to the reader to discover or infer the writer's purpose. These key questions will help the critical reader find the writer's purpose.

1. What is the writer's reason for making these statements?
2. What is the writer trying to convince me of or prove to me?

The following map is a summary of the major purposes used by writers.

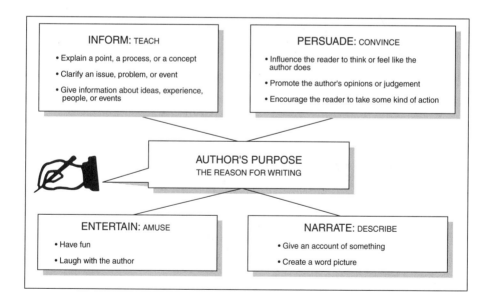

Read the following paragraph to decide the writer's purpose and then answer the question that follows.

The Western world got a new start in the centuries around 1500, and the core of that new beginning was a remarkable social and cultural revival we call the *Renaissance*. The word *renaissance* means "rebirth," and the period carrying that name, which began in Italy in the 1300s and climaxed across much of western Europe in the 1500s, has often been seen as the springtime of the modern world. Although this view has been challenged and reinterpreted by a number of historians over the past century and a half—and we will explore some of these objections—the fundamental strength of this conception justifies structuring this and the next chapter around the notion of a Western rebirth.

In the present chapter we deal with the aggressive "new monarchs" of the Renaissance who restored political power to the center of European states and with the economic expansion and social dynamism of the age as a whole. Then we turn to the great cultural achievements in thought and scholarship, literature and the arts for which the Renaissance is renowned. Later chapters in this part focus on other innovative, even revolutionary events that owe at least part of their impetus to this period of reawakening and rebirth.

Anthony Esler, *The Western World*

Circle your choice: What is the writer's purpose?

to inform   to persuade   to entertain   to narrate

A different form of critical reading involves the analysis of visual graphics. We will focus on this important aspect of textbook reading in the final chapter.

CHAPTER 6

The Value of Visual Aids

Learning from textbooks includes not only thinking critically about words but evaluating information from graphs, charts, diagrams, tables, illustrations, and photographs.

Visual literacy is important because much information can be condensed into a small amount of space. Moreover, visuals can dramatically show and summarize information. Business advertisements, for example, frequently compare products and use easy-to-read visuals to highlight the major selling points of a particular product. The media frequently use visuals, such as weather maps and tables, for comparison purposes.

Effectively reading your college textbooks often means integrating a substantial amount of visual information with printed information. Tables, charts, diagrams, and graphs are included in textbooks to give you important information in condensed form. The illustrations often try to help you understand difficult concepts presented in the text in a simpler format. If you overlook "reading" visual aids, you are ignoring a valuable source of information.

Graphics are expensive to reproduce and are included in your textbook for several important reasons. They

clarify concepts that are difficult to understand.
take the place of text in illustrating ideas or information.
add information to the text.

To read graphics critically, you should consider the source of the data and how current the information is. Usually, the source is included at the bottom of the graphic or in a footnote. *Read* the graphic as you would information in a passage, looking for the main idea or key point and the *relationship* of the supporting statements. Then compare the graphic to the information printed in the textbook.

Although reading visual information is not the same as reading prose, similar strategies can be used. Looking over a graph initially to get an overall idea is comparable to previewing written text; examining facts and putting them together can be compared to getting the main idea; and noting trends, patterns, and relationships can be compared to making inferences and drawing conclusions. It is also possible to apply the information, where appropriate, to yourself and your life-style.

As you will note in each section that follows, each type of visual requires a distinct reading strategy.

GRAPHS

Most often, graphs present statistics or quantities that are compared to one another by the use of bars, lines, or circles. In looking at the graph, the reader has to analyze the comparisons given. Often times, reading the title enables the reader to deduce the main point. Since the major purpose of graphs is to show *relationships*, the reader makes inferences and draws conclusions on the basis of these relationships. Graphs consists of three types: the bar, the line, and the circle or pie graph.

Bar and Line Graphs

Bar and line graphs have the same underlying structure, as shown in Figure 6.1

1. Both types of graphs have two lines drawn at right angles.
2. Each of these lines is referred to as an *axis*.
3. Each axis shows a measure of something.

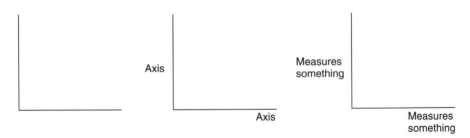

Figure 6.1   The Two Axes of a Graph Show Measures.

Bar Graphs

The following bar graph shows the relationship between three regions and how they changed over time.

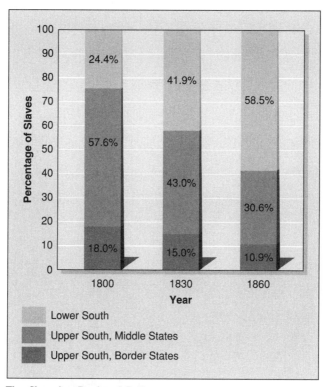

The Changing Regional Pattern of Slavery in the South, 1800–1860. As the nineteenth century progressed, slavery increasingly became identified with the cotton-growing Lower South

Bar graphs often include more than one bar. Dots or stripes or even color, can add to their impact. Bars can be placed either vertically (arranged from top to bottom) or horizontally (arranged from side to side), as can be seen in the previous graph and Figure 13–2 that compare the resources of the North and South in 1861 and the relative strength in seven categories of the combatants in WWI.

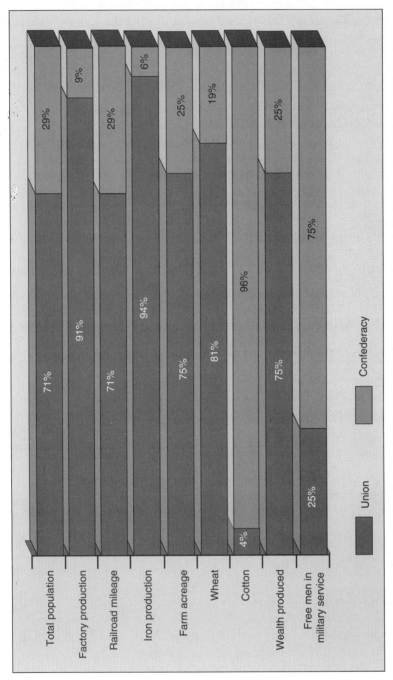

Comparative Resources, North and South, 1861   By 1865, the North's overwhelming advantage in population, industrial strength, railroad mileage, agriculture, and wealth was decisive in the final victory. But initially these strengths made little difference in a struggle that began as a traditional war of maneuver in which the South held the defensive advantage. Only slowly did the Civil War become a modern war in which all of the resources of society, including the property and lives of civilians, were mobilized for battle.

Source: *The Times Atlas of World History* (New Jersey: Hammond, 1978).

Legend: ▮ Union   ▮ Confederacy

Category	Union	Confederacy
Total population	71%	29%
Factory production	91%	9%
Railroad mileage	71%	29%
Iron production	94%	6%
Farm acreage	75%	25%
Wheat	81%	19%
Cotton	4%	96%
Wealth produced	75%	25%
Free men in military service	25%	75%

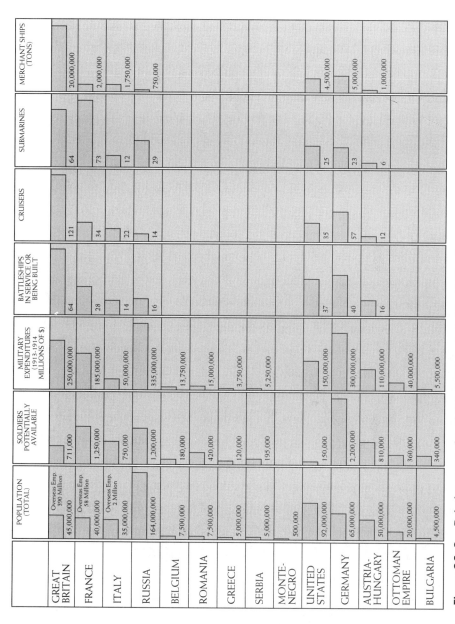

Figure 26–2 Relative strengths of the combatants in World War I.

Line Graphs

In examining line graphs, readers need to focus their attention on whether trends are moving upward or downward. With a line graph, the relationship between two or more items is shown by a line (or several lines) plotted and then drawn on the graph. Note how the following graphs dramatize how American personnel and bomb tonnage outpaced the Royal Air Force from 1943 until the end of the war.

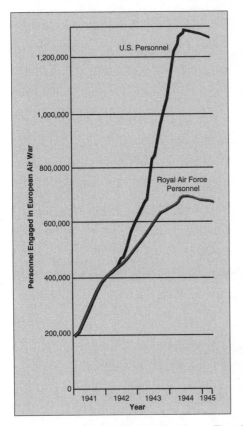 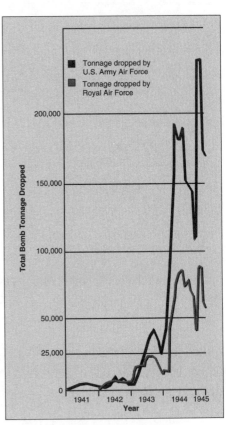

World War II: Personnel and Bombs   The offensive phase of the Allied campaign against the Axis unfolded late in the war. Major defeats in the Soviet Union and Africa deprived Germany of the resources needed to expand the war. The British and Americans, with an almost endless supply of materials and personnel, proceeded to overpower Germany and its European allies. Germans had ruled the skies early in the war. By 1943, Allied planes destroyed the German and Italian systems of transportation and supply, making cities almost unlivable. As British and Americans troops continued to pour into Europe, victory became inevitable.

Circle or Pie Graphs

Circle graphs divide a quantity of something into its parts. When the parts are measured in percentages, the entire circle graph or pie equals 100 percent. When fractions are used, the whole equals 1. Pieces of the "pie" show relative size, magnitude, or frequency of occurrence. The larger the pie wedge, the bigger fraction of the total is obviously represented.

The following pie graph shows the percentage of women engaged in various occupations in Massachusetts in 1837.

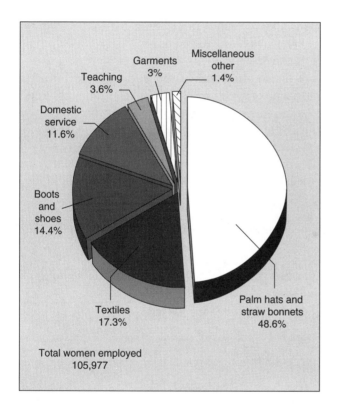

Occupations of Women Wage Earners in Massachusetts, 1837 This chart shows how important outwork was for women workers. Textile work in factories occupied less than 20 percent of women, while outwork in palm-leaf hats, straw bonnets, and boots and shoes accounted for over half of the total work force. Teaching was a new occupation for women in 1837. The small percentage of 3.6 would grow in the future. **Source:** Based on Thomas Dublin, *Transforming Women's Work* (Ithaca, N.Y.: Cornell University Press, 1991), table 1.1, p. 20.

How to Read Graphic Information

1. First, carefully read and think about the title and subtitles when given. This gives you the purpose of the graph and, therefore, tells you what you can expect to learn from it. Turn the title into a question. Ask: How, What, or Why.

2. Next, read the legend (or caption) to learn how to interpret the details presented. Sometimes the legend is at the bottom of the graph. For example, the legend may help to clarify whether the numbers are in thousands, millions, or billions.
3. Check for other explanatory notes. These might include explanation of abbreviations and information on how the data was collected or may indicate whether the data is incomplete.
4. Then, skim the information up and down the vertical column ($\updownarrow$) as well as the information across the horizontal column ($\leftrightarrow$) for bar and line graphs. You will sometimes have to approximate the numbers; the bars or lines of many graphs fall between the numbers given. Find out what units of measurement have been used.
5. Write a sentence, answering the question you posed in Step 1.
6. Finally, determine the relationship of the information shown in the horizontal and vertical columns. Understanding this relationship is the key to reading not only graphs but tables, charts, and some diagrams.
7. Ask yourself some key questions to understand the graphics.
   a. What general information is presented, and for what purpose?
   b. What relationship has been plotted?
   c. What inferences and conclusions can be made?

In making your inferences and drawing conclusions, ask yourself these questions:

Is the source of the data reliable?
How were the data gathered?
Is there any bias in how the data are presented?

Examine the following graph, applying the key questions.

   a. General information and purpose:

   _____

   _____

   b. Relationship/s shown:

   _____

   _____

   c. Inferences and conclusions:

   _____

   _____

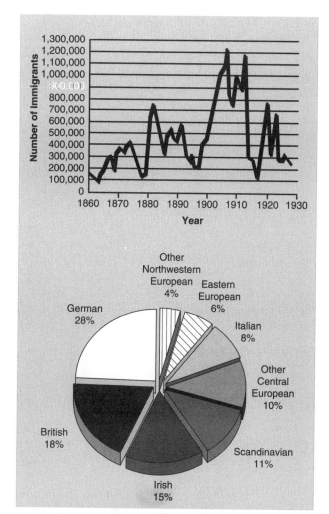

Immigration to the United States, 1860–1929   The peak years of immigration in the last half of the nineteenth century were 1873, 1882, and 1892, each also marking the beginning of an economic recession. Immigration slowed when jobs were scarce, especially following the financial Panics of 1873 and 1893, and picked up again during periods of recovery.   **Source:** *Statistical Abstract of the United States, 1921 and 1930.*

Tables

Tables, too, are often used to show comparisons. The data is generally given in numbers and usually arranged in columns and rows with headings that explain what the numbers mean. The reader has to think about the comparisons being made and draw some conclusions based on whether any of the numbers are significantly larger or smaller than others and to decide what trends these conclusions suggest.

The following table details hazardous waste sites in the United States and includes both proposed and final sites of hazardous waste. Additionally, the table includes the number of sites in each state out of a total of 1207 and each state's percentage of the total.

Examine the table and answer the questions that follow.

Hazardous Waste Sites on the National Priority List, by State: 1990 [includes both proposed and final sites listed on the National Priorities List for the Superfund program as authorized by the Comprehensive Environmental Response, Compensation, and Liability Act of 1980 and the Superfund Amendments and Reauthorization Act of 1986]

State	Total Sites	Rank	Percent Distri-bution	State	Total Sites	Rank	Percent Distri-bution
Total	1,207	(x)	(x)	Missouri	24	15	2.0
United States	1,197	(x)	100.0	Montana	10	34	0.8
				Nebraska	6	43	0.5
Alabama	12	27	1.0	Nevada	1	50	0.1
Alaska	6	43	0.5	New Hampshire	16	22	1.3
Arizona	11	29	0.9				
Arkansas	10	34	0.8	New Jersey	109	1	9.1
California	88	3	7.4	New Mexico	10	34	0.8
				New York	83	4	6.9
Colorado	16	22	1.3	North Carolina	22	17	1.8
Connecticut	15	24	1.3	North Dakota	2	48	0.2
Delaware	20	19	1.7	Ohio	33	12	2.8
District of Columbia	—	(x)	—	Oklahoma	11	29	0.9
Florida	51	6	1.1	Oregon	8	40	0.7
				Pennsylvania	95	2	7.9
Hawaii	7	42	0.6	Rhode Island	11	29	0.9
Idaho	9	38	0.8	South Carolina	23	16	1.9
Illinois	37	10	3.1	South Dakota	3	46	0.3
Indiana	35	11	2.9	Tennessee	14	25	1.2
Iowa	21	18	1.8	Texas	28	13	2.3
Kansas	11	29	0.9	Utah	12	27	1.0
Kentucky	17	21	1.4	Vermont	8	40	0.7
Louisiana	11	29	0.9	Virginia	20	19	1.7
Maine	9	38	0.8	Washington	45	7	3.8
Maryland	10	34	0.8	West Virginia	5	45	0.4
Massachusetts	25	14	2.1	Wisconsin	39	9	3.3
Michigan	78	5	6.5	Wyoming	3	46	0.3
Minnesota	42	8	3.5	Guam	1	(x)	(x)
Mississippi	2	48	0.2	Puerto Rico	9	(x)	(x)

—Represents zero x Not applicable.

U.S. Environmental Protection Agency, press release, August 1990 *Statistical Abstract of the United States*, 1991

1. Which three states have the largest total number of sites?

_____

_____

2. Which three states have the lowest total number of sites?

_____

_____

3. Which three states have the highest concentration of hazardous waste in terms of percentage of the total?

_____

_____

4. Which three states have the lowest concentration of hazardous waste in terms of percentage of the total?

_____

_____

Diagrams

A diagram refers to some form of drawing with distinctive labeled parts. A diagram can be as simple as a line drawing or as complex as a causal analysis in a chemistry text. Diagrams can be used in diverse areas, from plotting how a plane flies to the stages an embryo goes through to become a fetus and eventually a newborn baby. In reading them, you have to think about what the various parts represent and how they can be tied together. Usually, the title or caption will provide the reader with the main idea, the relationship being illustrated. The reader must identify the main idea, find out its purpose, and understand what is implied within section or portion of the diagram.

Maps are a kind of diagram. Map 29–2 illustrates, in a graphic form different from a table, Harry Truman's margin of victory in the 1948 election.

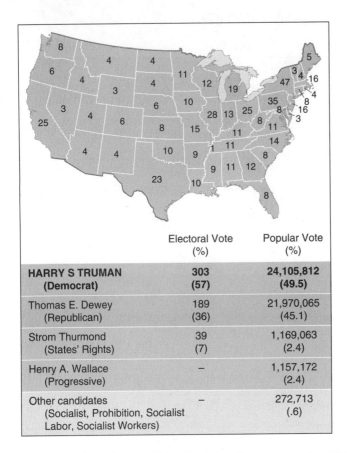

	Electoral Vote (%)	Popular Vote (%)
HARRY S TRUMAN (Democrat)	**303** **(57)**	**24,105,812** **(49.5)**
Thomas E. Dewey (Republican)	189 (36)	21,970,065 (45.1)
Strom Thurmond (States' Rights)	39 (7)	1,169,063 (2.4)
Henry A. Wallace (Progressive)	–	1,157,172 (2.4)
Other candidates (Socialist, Prohibition, Socialist Labor, Socialist Workers)	–	272,713 (.6)

Map 29-2   The Election of 1948   Harry Truman won a narrow victory in the presidential election of 1948 by holding many of the traditionally Democratic states of the South and West and winning key industrial states in the Middle West. His success depended on the coalition of rural and urban interests that Franklin Roosevelt had pulled together in the 1930s.

INTEGRATING TEXT AND GRAPHICS

When reading textbooks, you will often need to integrate the information in graphics and text. Sometimes, what you read is clarified or explained in a graphic, but other times the graphic simply adds more information to the text. You will need to go back and forth, integrating both sets of information. Some instructors refer to this as "two-finger" reading; that

is, you hold your place in the text while reading the graphic, moving back and forth through a chapter.

You are now on your own. As you begin to study from your History textbook, we encourage you to apply the strategies you have just learned to become an active reader and learner. You may need to modify some techniques because of a passage's contents but what you have learned here are the essential skills readers use to critically analyze and remember important information. Go to it!